# BEHIND THOSE DARK EYES

A COLLECTION OF
DEEP AND RAW POETRY

*D.J. Walters*

First published in Great Britain in 2020 by:
*WW*
Walters Way Publishing
www.djwalterswriter.com
djwalterswriter@gmail.com

Copyright © 2020 Dionne Jennene Walters
All rights reserved.

PUBLISHER'S NOTE
This is a work of poetic fiction. Names, characters, places and incidents are either the products of the author's imagination or are used fictitiously. Any resemblance to actual people, living or dead; events or locales are entirely coincidental.

Without limiting the rights under the copyright reserved above, no part of this publication may be reproduced, stored in or introduced into a retrieval system, or transmitted in any form, or by any means (electronic, mechanical, photocopying, recording or otherwise), without the prior written permission of both the copyright owner and the above publisher of the book.

The scanning, uploading and distribution of this book via the internet or via any other means without the permission of the publishers is illegal and punishable by law. Please purchase only authorised electronic editions and do not participate in or encourage electronic piracy of copyrighted materials. Your support of the author's rights are appreciated.

While the author has made every effort to provide accurate contact numbers and addresses (including websites and emails) at the time of publication, neither the publisher nor the author assume any responsibility for errors, or for changes that occur after publication. Furthermore, the publisher does not have any control over and does not assume any responsibility for author or third-party websites or their content.

This book is sold subject to the condition that it shall not, by way of trade or otherwise, be lent, re-sold, hired out or otherwise circulated without the publisher's prior consent in any form of binding or cover other than that in which it is published and without a similar condition including this condition being imposed on the subsequent purchaser.

Catalogue record for the publication data:

ISBN-13: 978-1-9999276-7-7
Behind Those Eyes by D.J. Walters
Fiction- Poetry- Adult Poetry

Manufactured and Printed by Ingram Spark
www.ingramspark.com

# BEHIND THOSE DARK EYES

A COLLECTION OF
DEEP AND RAW POETRY

WALTERS WAY PUBLISHING

# OTHER TITLES BY D.J. WALTERS

The Vacation Lodge

The Vacation Lodge II

The Vacation Lodge III

For Melissa;

~Your realness is unmatched~

The one who's held witness to my deepest of wounds

The keeper of all of my deepest of secrets

The one who accepts me for who I am

# REVIEWS

"Walters creates a space for vulnerability…to witness the beauty of the human experience in its rawest form"
-Caleb Femi- Author of 'Poor'-

"Amazing, Raw, Truthful"
-Apple Whilby-

"Seductive, educational and real"
-Jocelyn Gregory-

"An amazing, insightful and therapeutic read"
-L. Shah-

"Evokes a rollercoaster of emotions as well as deep rooted memories"
-J. Browne-

"I got the chance to dive deeper… and connect on a different level"
-S. Williams-

"Thought provoking but empowering and authentically beautifully written… a poetry book that keeps on giving"
-S. Breatcliffe-

# BEHIND THOSE DARK EYES

A COLLECTION OF
DEEP AND RAW POETRY

---

# CONTENTS

## ON THE MIND — 1

| | |
|---|---|
| *BEHIND THOSE DARK EYES* | 2 |
| *WHEN DOES THE MIND SLEEP?* | 4 |
| *SOMETIMES, I JUST WANT TO GIVE UP* | 6 |
| *LONELINESS* | 8 |
| *THE PURGE* | 10 |
| *DEAR GOOGLE* | 12 |
| *FILLING THE VOID* | 14 |
| *UNDER WATER* | 15 |
| *SAPIOSEXUAL* | 16 |
| *RIPEN WITH AGE* | 17 |
| *IS EDUCATION THE KEY TO SUCCESS?* | 18 |
| *POWER WITHIN* | 20 |
| *GOALS* | 21 |
| *MARIJUANA 'ROUND THE CORNER* | 22 |
| *RATS IN THE KITCHEN* | 24 |
| *SOCIAL ANXIETY* | 25 |
| *THE POWER OF THOUGHT* | 26 |
| *BIGGEST FEAR* | 28 |
| *HIGHS AND LOWS* | 30 |
| *ADDICTED TO POETRY* | 31 |

## ON THE BODY 33

| | |
|---|---|
| *My Skin Tells a Story* | 34 |
| *I am not Black* | 36 |
| *Melanin Drips* | 38 |
| *Her-moans* | 39 |
| *Stretch Marks* | 40 |
| *Broken Pussy* | 42 |
| *Please Don't Touch Me (There)* | 43 |
| *Dear Melanated Woman,* | 44 |
| *Dear Melanated Man,* | 47 |
| *You forgot* | 50 |
| *Dis(ease)* | 51 |
| *Our Lives Matter* | 52 |
| *Pan African* | 54 |
| *Body Dysphoria* | 56 |
| *It Itches* | 58 |
| *Imperfections* | 59 |
| *Be Careful* | 60 |
| *My Curl is Different to Your Curl* | 62 |
| *The Body is our Temple* | 64 |
| *The Heart that Beats Tirelessly* | 65 |

## ON THE SOUL 67

| | |
|---|---|
| *Trapped* | 68 |
| *Is there a God?* | 70 |
| *When Will I Be Free?* | 72 |
| *Soul Mates* | 73 |
| *Fate* | 74 |
| *Is the Grass Greener?* | 76 |
| *Plants Have Feelings Too* | 77 |

| | |
|---|---:|
| *MIRROR, MIRROR* | **78** |
| *THOSE STREETS* | **79** |
| *COLEBY PATH* | **82** |
| *DON'T WORRY LITTLE GIRL* | **84** |
| *A BLESSING AND A CURSE* | **86** |
| *YOU ARE WHAT YOU EAT* | **87** |
| *NEGATIVE ENERGY* | **89** |
| *E=MC²* | **90** |
| *WHY CAN'T WE LIVE IN SIMPLICITY?* | **91** |
| *WHEN I DIE* | **92** |
| *RESET* | **93** |
| *THERE ARE TWO TYPES OF PEOPLE* | **94** |
| *RE-BIRTH* | **95** |

## ON SEX & RELATIONSHIPS 97

| | |
|---|---:|
| *FIRST LOVE* | **98** |
| *HEARTBREAK* | **100** |
| *LOVE BITES* | **102** |
| *LIFE PARTNER* | **103** |
| *UNDER THE RUG* | **104** |
| *IT HURTS* | **106** |
| *IS THIS REALLY WHAT I WANT?* | **107** |
| *I JUST WANT THE D* | **108** |
| *THE ONE* | **110** |
| *SIXTY-NINE* | **111** |
| *WILL I EVER BE GOOD ENOUGH?* | **112** |
| *YOU CHEATED ON ME* | **113** |
| *MY SWEET VALENTINE* | **114** |
| *BEST FRIENDS* | **116** |
| *THOSE HANDS* | **118** |
| *VITAMIN S* | **119** |

| | |
|---|---:|
| *SMOOTH LIKE BUTTER* | **120** |
| *GIVE ME KNOWLEDGE* | **121** |
| *A ROYAL FLUSH* | **122** |
| *RELATIONSHIP GOALS* | **124** |

## ON FAMILY & FRIENDS      127

| | |
|---|---:|
| *A PEACOCK IN THE JUNGLE* | **128** |
| *A FRIEND FOR EACH FINGER* | **130** |
| *SLEEPOVERS* | **131** |
| *SHOOBS* | **132** |
| *JEALOUSY* | **134** |
| *WERE YOU THERE?* | **135** |
| *TRUE FRIENDS* | **136** |
| *FAKE FRIENDS* | **137** |
| *BETRAYAL* | **138** |
| *WHEN FRIENDS BECOME FAMILY* | **139** |
| *FRIENDSHIP GOALS* | **140** |
| *BLOOD IS THICKER THAN WATER* | **141** |
| *SISTERLY LOVE* | **142** |
| *BEST COUSINS* | **144** |
| *DADDY'S GIRL* | **146** |
| *BROKEN HOME* | **148** |
| *BITTER SWEET MOTHER* | **150** |
| *THE MATRIARCH* | **153** |
| *GRANDAD: A MAN OF DISTINCTION* | **155** |
| *A LETTER TO MY FUTURE CHILD* | **157** |

# FOREWARD

Dive into this ocean of deep and raw poetry. A captivating collection of works written to capture the most intimate parts of the human psyche. Authentically and intricately crafted from behind the dark eyes of the writer, this compilation presents a taste of the melanated, female experience. Though unpopular and at times, politically incorrect, this collection comprises of ideas that challenge the mind, the body, the soul and works to explore the unequivocal and explicit truths behind family, friends, sex and relationships. If you've been wounded by the harsh realities of life, there's bound to be a poem for you. If you've loved and want to be loved the right way, it's time to explore the sapiosexual in you. This collection is for all those who've suffered and been left with battle scars; and for all those yearning to re-ignite the dying spark that's faintly glowing inside; know that you are not alone. Come on in and let's all heal together.

# ON THE MIND

## *Behind Those Dark Eyes*

Waking up at the crack of dawn,

With a million thoughts.

None are of sense

There's crack in that tap.

Bang! Gun shots fire in my head.

The fear of a knife stabbing through my eye.

And of a child's innocence in my culpable hands.

The grip that's too heavy.

The strangle too tight.

Grabbing hold of myself.

But they keep coming back.

Flashes of childhood haunting my soul.

Tears from a mother all out of control.

Hysterical laughter for no reason at all.

And unstable uncles acting a fool.

There's food in your beard. What is that smell?

The urge to scream in a public place.

The surge of frustration with their ever-so-slow pace.

Bursting out in a song just because I choose.

Having bouts of mania then back to recluse.

Because you bore me.

You don't stimulate me enough.

Yet my thoughts keep talking and I talk back.

I listen too much. Too hard.

Then I counter act,

Just to fit in.

But behind gritted teeth, I plaster on a smile.

I regain composure and the thoughts subside.

And that's not even half of what's behind those dark eyes.

# *When Does The Mind Sleep?*

Does the mind sleep when your eyes close?

Or does it sleep when you zone into your favourite television shows?

Does the mind sleep when you drive from A and wake up at B?

Or does it sleep at the mistakes you choose not to see?

Does the mind sleep in those long meetings you learned nothing from?

Or does it sleep when that loved one's voice nags on?

Does your mind sleep when you enter a room and forget why you're there?

Or does it sleep when you're dancing without a smidget of care?

Does your mind sleep when you start a snack and can't figure out how it finished?

Or does it sleep when you give up and your soul is diminished?

Does your mind sleep the night that your work's due?

Or does it sleep before your results?

Does it sleep when you know the answer?

Does it sleep when you've cleared the debt?

Does it sleep when you've still got dishes in the sink?

Does it sleep in all of the mess?

## ~ 5 ~

Does your mind sleep when you run from your fears in dream land?
Or does it sleep on the nights you can't remember your dreams?
Does the mind sleep on those nights where you "only just closed your eyes"?
Does the mind sleep when you have a quick 30-minute nap?

Does the mind sleep when you're shattered?
Does the mind sleep when you're alert?
Does it sleep when you hit snooze?
Does it sleep when you relax?
When does the mind sleep?

## *Sometimes, I Just Want to Give Up*

Life isn't always a bed full of lilies.
Sometimes the thorns stab you in the back.
It's not always easy to pull out the nettles and sludge from the mud that's holding you back.

Sometimes the snakes dress up like butterflies,
Or they hide between the grass.
And you can't find the strength to smear a smile on your face when they bite you in the ass.

Sometimes you have to take a step back to move forward,
And the revision feels like a drone.
Sometimes you pretend like you've got it all covered to disguise all of your tiresome groans.
Sometimes you're dragged down, deep into the earth,
And you can't seem to find a way out.

Sometimes you're kicked down and they stand in your way.
Sometimes you're shut up and have nothing to say.
Sometimes you go left when you should've gone right.
And that's when you have to think twice as hard just to work your way around with all of your might.

Sometimes, I just want to give up.

Close the door. Shut off from the world.

Tuck my head under the duvet. Clutch my knees to my chest.

I just want to stay under there forever and not come back out.

Close my eyes and not wake back up.

But something buried deep inside always whispers in my ear:

You have so much more to give.

Your story has just begun.

And I'm not done with you yet.

# *Loneliness*

Loneliness is:

Being in a room filled with people and feeling as if no one is there.

Having news you want to share but feeling no one wants to hear.

Not bothering because no one else is bothered.

The recognition that nobody can make it to the birthday celebration you planned.

Having 10 invitations but feeling welcome at none.

That urge to go out with nowhere to go.

Wanting to share experiences but having no one to share it with.

Missing out on that movie, that weekend away, that once-in-a-lifetime event and getting a table for one.

Having friends that don't ask how you are.

Feasting on 565 likes on social media to fill the emptiness inside.

Writing on their wall just so that you can be seen.

Updating your feed to the point where even you don't know your status.

Seeing plenty of fish but catching none though you could have sworn blind that your net had swiped right that time.

Repeatedly opening and closing the same four applications just to look busy,

Or to fall asleep.

That endless scroll.

That deafening ring you hear in your ears when you stare into space.

That mind-numbing hum.

Loneliness is:

That clogged-up ignition.

That lack of drive.

A choked car when it stalls.

A road block.

A mind block.

A block.

A bitch.

## *The Purge*

I see it. I want it.

No questions asked.

I've already convinced myself.

I can't hold back the urge.

They look so damn good and they're calling my name.

So I dive in.

And in. And in.

And keep going back for more.

And when I'm almost done, I need just one more.

Aaahhh finally...

My cheeks fill with joy.

My urge satisfied.

Then I sit back.

My stomach bloated to the max.

The breath in my lungs transformed into gas.

As a matter of fact,

I have no space to breathe.

So I look in the mirror.

My midriff protrudes.

It protrudes so much, it can barely move

And it's as hard as a rock.

I feel so fuckin' fat.

My head fills with regret.
My mind fills with doubt.
My once filled cheeks drop.
And the tears fill my eyes.
I shouldn't have done that.
I can't face myself.
My feet rush through the door.
Fingers forced down my throat.

And that's when I purge.
Bluuuuurrrgghh!

# *Dear Google*

Who started the First World War?

Why was there a World War Two?

What is the purpose of a Monarchy?

How do you coach surf?

Can you be vegan and pregnant?

How do you grow a vegan baby?

Why does the skin around your nails peel?

Why do Drake and Kanye have beef?

What are the symptoms of Lordosis?

What is the Harry potter theme song?

How do you cleanse your colon?

What types of potatoes are there?

Can you cook Avocadoes?

Why do we overeat?

How deadly are Nightshades?

What do falling dreams mean?

Why do we never die in our dreams?

Why do children repeat questions over and over again?

What's the best way to make money from home?

What are the best cheap dates?

What are Scorpio's star sign compatibilities?

Why do opposites attract?

Why does my stomach bloat?

How many farts does the average person do in a day?

How many poops are normal?

## ~ 13 ~

How fast does hair grow on your head?

When does hair stop growing?

Why does hair turn grey?

How many thoughts does a human have in a day?

Thanks in advance.

## *Filling the Void*

I eat when I'm bored.

I eat when I'm excited.

I eat when I'm stressed.

I eat when I'm depressed.

I eat when I'm hungry.

I eat when I'm peckish.

I eat when I'm full.

I eat when I'm reading.

I eat when I'm scared.

I eat when I'm watching.

I eat when I'm not.

I eat just in case.

And if I don't,

I feel empty,

And lost.

So I must eat,

Just to

Fill

That

Void.

## *Under Water*

They ask, "How are you?"

And I say, "Fine," with a pleasant smile.

No one really wants to hear how you are.

No one wants to hear you've been taken hostage by your thoughts.

And I don't think they actually care.

No one wants to hear about the voices,

The screams and the visions that challenge your sanity.

No one wants to hear that you're drowning

And no one really understands what they can't see.

So when I say "and you?" they glow because it's their turn to let it all out.

Whilst my head sinks underwater.


I sit there and nod and smile but their voices muffle into one.

I can't make out what they're saying

Because I'm in a world of my own.

The vision of them is blurred

And the waft of the water filters them out.

And even when I try to lift my head up again,

It feels heavy; the pressure's too much.

I just can't join in.


But under water my tears blend in.

So they can't see it but I'm struggling.

One day, I'll figure it out.

## *Sapiosexual*

I want your thoughts;

To penetrate deeply into my mind.

To caress my soul and soothe my inner desires.

To provoke and summon my senses.

To transport me to new heights of arousal.

To wrap me up like a quilted blanket.

To rouse me from a stagnant sleep.

To lead me down a winding path.

To hoist me into your lucrative labyrinth.

To finger the depths of my psyche

To come all over mine.


I want to;

Explore your fairground.

Seep deep into your understanding.

Softly stroke your enthralling emotions.

Lick between your intellectual lobes.

Taste the secretions of your subconscious.

Gently galvanize your demeanour and roughly rile your behaviour.


Let your words fuck with mine and create beautiful babies.

Let's interlock in old theories and make a breed of our own.

Thrash into my concepts and build empires with in.

Leave the rest at the door and let only them come on in.

I just want your thoughts.

## *Ripen With Age*

I never fear getting another year older
Because for me, I ripen with age.
Each year feels even sweeter
And I can never wait to pick up the pace.

It's the perfect excuse to explore all the things
I never got to the year before.
It's a new possibility to meet new minds
That challenge and open mine some more.

An extra year makes room for growth
And also learning from mistakes.
And each time I get better and better
At identifying the real from the fake.

Another year is another opportunity
To seek knowledge and act upon it.
And each year is a few or more steps
Closer to my goals.

Another year is another chance to right my wrongs
And heal my past.
I'm always thankful for another year
Because it's always better than my last.

## *Is Education the Key to Success?*

Education is the key to success! The message that has been relayed
to populations of people worldwide.
Somehow, the human species have come to a general consensus that
this statement is true!
On a national scale, the schooling establishments which achieve the
highest grades by their students are celebrated on the news.
And the whole society is exposed to this.
So high grades are seen by many as a clear measure of success.

So parents tell their children they must get a good education
in order to be a success.
Some start school from the precious age of four
And their teachers relay the same message.
They get praise for high grades, following instructions
And working hard and even their peers congratulate this.
So the indoctrination has started.
So doing well at school is the key to your success.
And the parents who believe this tell their children
that good qualifications are needed for success.

So they teach them to sit still, follow instructions,
work quietly and to never answer back.
And the ones who speak out and challenge the rules
are punished and that is a fact.
Punished in school and then in society for utilising one's own mind.

So they become successful at following rules
and regurgitating the facts the teacher's find.
So after 18 long years of indoctrination,
They are ready for the work place.
They are ready to live by someone else's rules
without spitting in their face.

Is that success? Well let's have a look at what success really is.
Success is achieving your dreams and desires;
Some of which may not fit in the norms of this.
So if being a superhero makes you happy,
Then you have reached success.
And if being a top paid lawyer brings you all the joy,
well then, you have done your best.

Now don't get me wrong, education enhances knowledge of self and
society, and that is extremely important.
But the wrong education can stifle individuality, creativity
and one's belief in one's self.
Learning can happen anywhere with anyone
and not just in a school building.
Evaluating and applying the skills
From every situation you are placed in.
So if anyone ever asks is education the key,
my answer is always yes.
Because acquiring knowledge to be the best that you can be
Is the real key to all success.

---

**BEHIND THOSE DARK EYES** | *On The Mind*

## *Power Within*

On an average day, we use only a percentage of our brain.

Imagine all the power that's untapped within.

Imagine transcending our thoughts so that others could hear

Or so that we could indeed listen.

Imagine moving things with your mind like Matilda

Or in fact moving mountains.

Imagine unleashing the superhero in you

And saving generations.

Imagine travelling back in time to heal your past

So you could thrive in your present.

Imagine gaining control over what you thought you couldn't.

Imagine conquering all your fears.

Imagine having super healing powers

That made you and your family look younger than your years.

Imagine having a super memory

So you could easily acquire knowledge.

Imagine being capable of anything

And having everything that you wanted.

Imagine transforming night dreams into reality.

It's actually scary when you think about it.

How deep is our untapped ability?

How deep are our fears and our gifts?

Do we really only use just a percentage of our brain,

Or

Is this just a myth?

## *Goals*

The best goals are scored with the tunnel-visioned mind.
Where you see nothing else but the complete picture on the other side.
Blacking out all the rest and aiming only to score.
That terminator attitude where nothing stops you from getting what you set out for.
Obstacles are temporary road blocks.
When you're blocked, you always say "Well, I'll be back,"
'Cos nothing or no one can divert you off track.
It's those little steps every day.
It's those sacrifices you take.
It's getting up while you're asleep.
And staying awake.
Even when all you hear is 'no' and negative self-talk gets you depressed,
It's turning 'whys?' to 'why nots?' and 'nos' into 'yes.'
It's looking back on the way and seeing how far you've come.
At all the battles you've faced and all the battles you've won.
It's that adrenaline rush.
It's that pat on the back.
It's that fist hugged in your chest.
Those spasms of silent claps
That you give to yourself
When you smash through the net.
It's that feeling alone that makes it all worth it.

**BEHIND THOSE DARK EYES** | *On The Mind*

## *Marijuana 'Round the Corner*

Marijuana 'round the corner.
In the school toilets.
Rolling up to wind down,
And crack a joke of no sense.

Marijuana 'round the corner,
In the alley between the gates.
Choke on the fumes as they light,
And they fly to their brains,
For that buzz that trembles underneath the skin.
And as that buzz vibrates it causes a numbing within,
'Till you can't feel your top lip and you wonder where it went.

You wonder if they've noticed too with all the time that you've spent.
They're all staring at you.
And now you know why.
Your top lip is missing and you believe you can fly.
You're all zombified.
You find snacks to munch.
You eat. You're not hungry.
It's just that 'Juana from Cunch.
You're home and you've forgotten how you even got there.

You put it down to your wings and hope that they do not care.
Your thoughts are on 100. You wonder if they can tell,
that you're as high as a kite and feeling hot as hell.
You sink into your bed and it swallows you up.
You can't figure out why you're sinking so much.

Your mind spins and swirls.
You get the shivers and shakes.
Your eyes are wide shut.
Your heart palpitates.
Way into the next day.
You can't tell your parents.
But you swear you'll never puff 'round the corner again.

## *Rats in the Kitchen*

There's rats in the kitchen.

They're scratching.

I'm itching.

Their scuttles keep me awake.

And just when I think I'm about to fall asleep,

I shoot up in fear that one will crawl on my face.

My lids whip open at every single sound.

And I listen so hard, I can hear my quivering heart pound.

The squeaks haunt me.

I hear rushes past my ear.

My eyes are red from searching for holes to block in there.

I can't sleep.

I won't sleep.

So I rock in bed.

Pins and needles prickle through my head.

Pins and needles prickle through my head.

When

Oh when will it stop?

## *Social Anxiety*

Eyes wide.

Room filled.

Licks lips.

Lips peel.

Loud laughs.

Big stares.

Heart pounds.

Bites nails.

Small groups.

Tight chairs.

I'm late.

Go where?

Lip sweats.

Wet pits.

Looks left.

They're there.

Heart skips.

Rushed feet.

Moves swift.

Chest deep.

Slip in.

Lungs breathe,

"Hey."

# *The Power of Thought*

Thoughts are like seeds that are sprinkled in the mind.
Some pass by in the wind and some are planted.
And the more we focus on it, the deeper it gets,
And the roots of the thought start to grow and to spread.
This is great if it's a dream that needs to be fed
But, it's worse when it's a fear that is better off dead.

You are your thoughts.
You are your actions.
You are what is repeatedly said.
You are your fears.
You are your regrets.
You are the limits you set.

You are the driver.
You change the route.
You find the way out of the dead ends.
You are the hunger.
Feed your focus.
You are what you manifest.

You have the power to cross out the noughts over and over again.
You have the power to keep crossing 'till you believe you can win.
You have the power to decide what's planted
And, what passes in the wind.

## ~ 27 ~

You have the power to water seeds daily and let the buds flourish.

You have the power to uproot the weeds and throw them in the bin.

You have power over your thoughts;

Even the ones that seem over-powering.

## *Biggest Fear*

Franklin Roosevelt once said, "The only thing we have to fear is fear itself."
Fear is that tiny voice in the back of your head,
That haunts you and tells you you're no good.
Fear will convince you of all the reasons why you shouldn't,
When there is only one reason why you should.

Fear gives you unparalleled speed
You never even knew existed inside of you;
So you can run away from a problem
Without it catching you.

It's funny because the instinct of fear is meant to protect you from harm;
It's meant to keep you safe.
So it locks up your inhibition and boxes you in like a jail cell,
To keep you out of harm's way.

It keeps you safe from the risk you could have been in,
And the adventure you could have been on,
So that you don't get hurt.
But that same fear that's meant to aid you
Has the power to paralyse you from the neck down;
Just like that fatal car accident that could've knocked you for six.
Crushing your bones, your voice, your limbs,

Your heart, your mind and your spirit.

What kind of life is that?

One where we only watch others have fun

While we stay safely caged in.

A life of not putting in your all in case you fail

So coming third place instead of going for the win.

A life filled with "I wish I'd done that,"

Rather than filled with, "I wish I didn't."

A life filled with not trying and never taking a leap

Because of the tiny percentage of risk that you might tumble and fall.

I've always believed it's better to try and find out,

Rather than, to never try at all.

It's the experiences that shape you, they build character.

Life should indeed be lived.

With every experience comes a lesson,

a powerful message or something beautifully unexpected.

So when I think of my fears, it's not spiders or dogs

Or not having multitudes of wealth.

It's a life full of could-a's and not discovering the unknown.

My biggest fear is, in fact, fear itself.

## *Highs and Lows*

Some days, I feel on top of the world.

Some days, I want to sink.

Some days, nothing can bother me.

Some days, I'm bothered within.

Some days, I have so much to say.

Some days, I have nothing at all.

Some days, I stretch out proudly.

Some days, I'm in a ball.

Some days, I laugh to my heart's content.

Some days, my face is blank.

But what gets me through those dark days,

Is all the blessings I can thank.

## *Addicted to Poetry*

I am officially addicted to poetry.
I am addicted to freeing the mind.
I am addicted to self-expression.
I am addicted to seeing what I can find.

I am addicted to channelling my thoughts.
I am addicted to liberating within.
I am addicted to making sense of nonsense.
I am addicted to cleansing my sins.

I am addicted to healing my scars
I am addicted to the journey I've travelled so far.

I am addicted to solving the problems.
I am addicted to finding the clues.
I am addicted to self-discovery.
I am addicted to sharing it with you.

# ON THE BODY

## *My Skin Tells a Story*

My skin tells a story;
Of old and of new; of past and of present; of trauma and hurt.
Each mark is a sentence that makes up a chapter from a crucial event before each page is turned.

My skin tells a story;
Of a growing tomboy with scrapes and scratches from climbing the wall;
Of burns from a mother, in rush and in bother, me running for cover, a hot bath I recall;
Of shrivelled up thumbs from sucking too long;
My comfort, my blanket for keeping me strong;
Of operations, of sibling fights, of chicken pox, of acne spots.
Of left over hymen from virginity pops.
Of spots of beauty, of marks of birth and dimples that add to my shine.
Of rashes and reactions warning me to stop,
and pay attention to me and mine.

My skin tells a story; it's re-written every day.
A new tale for my evolving history that doesn't go away.
Though the scars fade, the memory lasts,
and just one look can take you right back,
to the time you were sick, the injection you had,
Or that haunting midnight attack.

## ~ 35 ~

Tattoos of adornment for the key moments,
and embellishment of the pain
of a past I'd rather forget or erase,
and just start all over again.

A fresh, blank slate.
Don't you just love a new page?
But if those marks never happened,
Would you still be the same?

## *I am not Black*

You told me you owned me,
And you did.
You told me to obey you,
So I did.
You told me to work,
So I did.
You told us to separate,
So we did.

You told me I weren't good enough,
So I believed it.
You told me my skin was too dark,
So I bleached it.
You told me my hair was too wild,
So I relaxed it.

You told me that my lips were too full,
My nose was too wide,
My thighs were too thick
And my bum was too big.
Well.... I couldn't change that...
You called me all sorts that I'd rather not repeat.
Because when I did, it made it okay for the whole world to say it.
Then you told me that I was Black

So I said;

"The Blacker the berry, the sweeter the juice."

"Black is beautiful."

"Black don't crack."

"I love Black love."

"I'm Black and I'm proud."

"Black people unite."

"Black lives matter."

You told me… "ALL lives matter."

So I said "MY life matters."


I am who I am.

I define my looks, my style, my shape, my thoughts and my beliefs.

I dance with rhythm;

I love bass and drums,

I eat healthful foods and we DON'T all eat fried chicken.

I don't fit in your box, so I cannot tick it.

Life is not black and white. There are shades to our image.


I am NOT a colour but I HAVE a colour.

And I'm not sure whether you've noticed or not,

But for those of you who haven't realised,

Black is one thing that I certainly am NOT.

## *Melanin Drips*

When I look at you, it's hard not to notice your skin.
It's so smooth, rich and shining and drips with melanin.
Your melanin drips like gold dust lighting this precious earth.
It drips the tears of your forefathers that strove and fought for us.
Your colour straps around you and protects you from the rays.
When it tears, it works even harder to prevent that tear again.
Your scars run deep and thick; they remind us of the hurt.
They are tattoos of war and remind us soldiers
That we can get up when we fall in the dirt.

Your hair and your eyes are dark and hold
Many o' wisdom-filled plights.
But that darkness helps you see the light
And blend into the dangers of the night.
And your bones are so dense and so strong,
So even when you're small, you're still big boned-ed.

And even when times get tough you just keep carrying on.
You absorb the light and it radiates within.
So when they say "I don't see colour," I know that they are lying.
Because your body is glowing and dripping
With rich,
Deep,
Sweet,
Melanin.

## *Her-moans*

Skin that's oily and shiny.
Like she's been dipped in a grease tin.
Hair in all the wrong places.
A woman with hairs on her chin.

Spots that are red, hurt and bumpy.
On her face, on her chest, on her back.
Breasts that are lumpy and humpy.
Like an overgrown cabbage patch.

Muscle that grows in her -gina.
Suffocating her -gina canal.
S-x that is painful and nauseous.
And it suffocates him as well.

Cysts that sprout like Brussels,
All over her ovaries.
When they burst, it hurts,
And they cause blood clots,
And excruciating bleeds.

And when it's almost her time,
The smallest thing makes her struggling eyes cry.
She smiles like a cat then barks like a dog
And no one really knows why.
Maybe it's just her-moans.

**BEHIND THOSE DARK EYES** | *On The Body*

## *Stretch Marks*

Stretch marks like tiger claws ripped through the meat of my back.
From all the meat I indulged that had slipped through the cracks,
And the pipes like a fiend, it kept calling me again.
'Till the pin worms transformed into fully fledged snakes,
That slithered from my hips all the way to my waist.
My waist, where the long-used leftovers lye.
Because in some parts of the world they're starved from morning 'till night.

I've never quite figured out the logic of how my full stomach serves them but in the hope of tips, I still wait.
I just can't leave the table until I've cleared the plate.
Childhood quotes haunting my adult thighs,
And haunting the greed that lies behind my dark eyes.
Time waits for no one, so I save every last scrap.
Stretch marks for the minor and major setbacks,
Where I try to regain control of my destiny though it seems a long stretch.

Stretch marks from the tribe that I represent.
Marks of ancestry and lineage from all the battles we've survived.
That stretch marks the spot of precious and cherished new lives.
Stretched to the limits just to make ends meet.
To protect your offspring 'till the winter has passed.
To withstand the cold as the storms never last.

Stretch marks the growth from that deep, planted seed.

That will flourish and grow from all of the foods that we feed.

Stretch marks the changes of time I failed to notice

When I fell, it wasn't always easy to get back up with successful focus.

You never really realise how far you've gone until you look back

At the steps on the path.

How I wish I'd looked out for all of my stretch marks.

## *Broken Pussy*

My pussy is broken.
It no longer works.
Every time we have sex, I tell you it hurts.

My walls are too dry;
They don't lubricate.
And my insides, they chafe,
When you penetrate.
I have lumps and growths in all the wrong places,
So it aches when we fuck on a regular basis.

My flaps are too long.
My hole is too wide.
And I barely can tell when your fingers inside.

My hairs are in-grown.
My periods are heavy.
My blood clots are thick.
I'm just never ready.

My Pussy is broken.
And infested with thrush.
That's why when you want sex, I'm not in a rush.

My Pussy is broken unfortunately,
Not the best part but it's part of me.

## *Please Don't Touch Me (There)*

It hurts. It's weird. It feels funny.

Our special tickling game where you touch me.

I love you and I know that you love me.

And I like it when you always call me pretty.

I promise one day that we'll marry.

And I really don't want to make you upset.

But our special game, I don't like it

My mummy said my private parts should be private.

But you told me that if tell, that mummy would get hurt.

And I really don't want her to come and blame me.

Now I dread when you have to look after me.

I don't want to be your special girl.

It doesn't seem right.

My other friends are my age.

I don't like our little secret.

This game isn't fun. I just want my mum.

Only the leaves in the trees take away my pain

I look up to the sky 'till it's over and done.


I don't want it to happen again.

I don't want my panties down.

I don't need those sleeping pills.

I don't want to wake up scared.

I don't want to kiss what is in your trousers.

And if you really care,

Please, can you just stop touching me (there).

**BEHIND THOSE DARK EYES** | *On The Body*

## *Dear Melanated Woman,*

Did you know we were made with intricate thought?
Did you know that your DNA has more value than those red bottoms you just bought?
You are the definition of regal.
You're nothing short of a Goddess.
You came from rich soil so we should expect nothing less.
So please fill me in. Tell me, what went wrong?
Somewhere along the line the truth got twisted, repeated
And then passed on.
And now we believe it.
Those twists are too hard to handle.
Those coils are too much to maintain.
But it's those twists and those tangles
Which create our remarkable mane.

You are a wonderful creature of nature
And even the wildest can be tamed.
Just like a forest, our crown grows towards the sun,
Our divine source of energy.
That's why our hair is full of life and vitality.
We don't need wigs or weave to 'protect' our beauty.

Our bush is not unprofessional because our style doesn't fit into the diaspora we were scattered into
Like the ashes from the dead.
The ashes from our buried history and our burnt kingdoms;

From a place we once called home.

Those ashes were scattered into a sea of darkness

Where we could no longer see anyone else that reflected our beauty.

We were blindfolded and gagged with a new narrative

That was force-fed.

It's no wonder we still walk around with a cover over our head.


But the only thing that needs to be straight

Are the words that come out of your mouth.

And that doesn't mean that we're aggressive if they can't handle the truth.

They're politically correct and we're correct in our truth.

You don't need to sit on the fence because they've taken offence.

Whose problem is it if they took it when it wasn't there to give?

Just like the rhythm in your hips, you can make your lips loose.

But we don't need to have a baby for every guy that we seduce.


Not everyone quite makes the mark and I'm sure you'll agree.

Is that one minute of pleasure worth a lifetime of struggling?

I know it's not always easy but I pray that we try our best to choose

The right one to procreate with so they can be in the child's life.

And not just on an insta-story or a post for a few likes.

A child deserves a role model from both sides who's more than a public figure on social media sites.

Just because it's in their bio, it doesn't make it real life.

---

**BEHIND THOSE DARK EYES** | *On The Body*

A child's life is just as precious as their experiences.

A child is not a trophy or a reward to be withheld or to give on the basis of our relationship status with the other half of them.

So let's not put what goes between our legs before

What comes out of them.

They have the right to both sides of the argument and the third side which is the truth.

Let them make a fair judgment without brainwashing or abuse.

Let's break the cycle that's been passed on from damaged lineages.

Let's remind them of who they can be and who they once were.

You are worthy, even when it's not reflected in mainstream media.

We don't need to compete against them or in fact, each other.

So don't be afraid to smile when you see someone

With the same reflection as you.

Your face is so much more attractive

When it's not fixed with a screw.

I know it's not always easy to show a lighter side when you're weighed down with life too.

Or when we're told we're strong, black, women when at times we feel weak too.

But we don't have to keep up the façade, if we don't want to

Because we are multifaceted creatures.

There's more than one setting in you.

So let go and be free.

P.S. I Love You.

## *Dear Melanated Man,*

You are the epitome of strength.

It's no wonder after the weight you've been carrying on your shoulders for centuries.

The weight of self-doubt can be a heavy burden to bear

And I know you've worked shifts,

Even after being told you're less than,

You are still trying to prove that you are a man.

When in reality, you don't have to.

You ooze it before you even speak.

You make men show respect and the ladies go weak.

You're not the runt of the litter, in fact, you are the Alpha.

You are courage and resilience. You are charisma. You are pride.

And you can be in touch with your feminine side.

Even when you try to hide it.

Sometimes that's cute. But sometimes it's a trip.

There's a thin line between being masculine and making it toxic.

Trying to protect your manhood and dispelling all the myths.

But you're more than bench-pressing beasts

And your big, black d—k.


And I know, my dear man that you're over tired from doing the most.

I can see it in your eyes.

But I just want you to know, that it's okay to cry sometimes.

It's okay to share your thoughts.

After all, you have the biggest pillows to cry on and the strongest rocks to lean on.

So it's okay to let go.

We are the female of you.

We're not competing for lead role,

We just want to produce with you.

Screen-write our future and edit out our mistakes.

Sit back and watch all of the cinematics take place.

But yet, after all of the whips, and the chains

And the ropes that you received in that dark place.

It seems that the things you ran from

Are the same things you now chase.

It's ironic.

You want The Big House, that land, that white picketed fence

With the wife to match.

You want that bright-light future in that house

While your history's out back.


The same female you came from, I pray that you rise her up.

If anyone knows her struggle it's you, the rest don't give a f--k.

Don't be pawn their game to confirm whether

"those rumours" are true.

Don't be the one that allows them to say the words

And do the things they really shouldn't do.

Protect and love your sisters. I pray that you love your own.

Just as much as you love others without putting them down.


There's already enough divide between us.

And I'm not even sure how it started.

Throwing shade at your sister because her shade doesn't fit.

It's ridiculous. We are the reflection of the magic melanin can create.

I just wish that you'd work your magic so we could all celebrate; together.

We don't need to prove points.

Put the competition to rest.

There is no reward for beating the tax man, being the hardest one out or having the longest staring contest.

We end up repping ends we don't own and end up killing our own.

We end up doing their job, when we could be doing our own

And believe it or not, there are more than three.

You are more than rap stars, trap stars and wannabe sport stars.

You are that dream that began before you hit puberty.

And beyond. You're magic. You are self-discovery.

They say the pen is mightier than the sword

But the mind is mightier than them both.

So use that entrepreneurial mind-set

To pass down something valuable to your own.

And please make it something more than just the materialistic.

'Cos there is no greater value than the gift of experiences.

Memories they can treasure forever, long after you're gone.

After all, the things you remember about childhood aren't the things you had

But what you done.


P.S. I've left some change to buy some trousers that fit.

I love you x.

---

**BEHIND THOSE DARK EYES** | *On The Body*

## *You forgot*

They say it's better to forgive and forget
But that's easier said than done.
First you forgot to turn off the stove,
So I turned it off and we got on.
Then you forgot to lock the door,
So I locked it and there was no harm done.

Then you forgot your keys at work again;
The pattern had begun.
After that, you forgot my birthday,
So that day I was all alone.

You forgot our beloved anniversary.
Then you forgot your way home.
You forgot how to trust.
You forgot how to love.
You forgot how to work.
You forgot how to laugh.

You forgot my name.
Then you forgot who I was
And I couldn't forgive that one.
Now that made my heart bleed.

And I'll never forgive that forgetting dis(ease)
For taking you from me.

## *Dis(ease)*

It's so silent.

It creeps up in the night.

Robbing you blind of your very own life.

It feasts on your goodies and kicks up its feet.

And eats.

And eats.

And eats.

And eats.


The more it eats, the bigger it gets.

The louder, the stronger, the wider it gets.

'Till it stares right at you and laughs in your face.

'Cos it's you that keeps feeding it in your once beautiful place.

It mocks and ridicules. It cuts 'till you bleed.

But you're too tired. You're too weak.

You can't be bothered to take heed.

It shakes you to wake up but you're still asleep.


You hit snooze on your alarms.

So dis(ease) ate to vacate.

But you didn't realise until it was too late.

Everything was gone.

You had nothing left.


If only you'd woken up on time.

# *Our Lives Matter*

Our lives matter because we were the first.
We travelled nations and produced life that reflected all of us.
Our lives matter.
Our soil is rich like our melanin.
We're fast, fit and agile.
We have the strength of a thousand men.

Our lives matter because ever since the invasion by C.Columbus,
Our strengths were transformed into weaknesses
and then used against us.
Now you use those same strengths as an excuse for why you felt defenceless.
And had no other option but to prematurely kill and then bury us,
While you get off scot-free.
Mothers' hands up asking, "Why?" when our hands were up in the sky, before we were shot aggressively.
And you call us barbaric, but, I've always questioned it.

What's more barbaric?
Killing someone because you don't like their look,
Or not eating with a knife and fork.
Raping women to save your dying race
Or praising the sun for your life and giving it grace?
Is it barbaric to force feed?
Force feed the vision of you, as my saving grace, until I believe?

Bible bashing whilst bashing our backs 'till you made the wounds bleed.
All to prove that you had control over me.

I take pity and laugh.
It's always the runt of the litter that barks the loudest.
Picking a scrap for no reason just to be noticed,
At the detriment of us.
Now we're dropping like flies when the worlds needs us.
But we've been brainwashed for years,
So it's hard to get the stain out of the cycle.
Told we're ugly, we're useless and we're too dangerous.
So when we see each other or hear things,
We expect nothing less.

We're so divided, we make groups to protect us from us.
We're so divided, we share with you before we share with one of us.
Frayed like a live wire holding on to make all ends meet.
But when your ends meet my ends, its lights out for somebody.
Our minds are still infected with toxic masculinity.
Our wounds are still healing from the brutality.

It's still raw and we know that we've got work to do.
So when we say our lives matter, I don't want no "Me Too".
Because all of this shit didn't happen to you.

## *Pan African*

No matter how far we are scattered,
We're still cut from the same cloth.
Our variation is vast but our genes were built to last.
So I like to call us Adidas originals
Because we're still all in,

Despite the division, the hate and the suffering.
After centuries of oppression and captivity,
There is hope though there's still a long walk 'till we're free.
But we are brave hearts and sacred like Solomon's seal.
So when there is a battle to be faced,
We shall prevail and never surrender
Like our East African King and Queens.

There is always struggle before revolution of control
Over the 'Black' identity.
And though our ancient cities have been ruined
And lives were lost over land,
We're still rich in minerals and our bird still stands.
It's not about how we started because the end crowns the work.

We can shine like the black stars that we are;
Like the Gold in our coast, our value is more.
And for your 4.1.1 we're not just 4.1.9.
We can grind 24/7 while you work 9 to 5.
Call us entrepreneurs. The best that you've seen.

I still long for the day where we can be natural in peace

Like the green white green.

I still long for Harambee and Uhuru na umoja;

That's freedom and unity.

We want Hurriyyah, Nizam, Adalah

If that even exists.

The moon and stars to be ours,

In Liberty, Order and Justice.

Though it's not always obvious,

Progress, peace and prosperity runs through us like the Gambia.

Though we've been scattered like ashes,

I pray we wake up to one people, one goal and one us.

Because when we're divided, we fall.

But when we're untied, we stand.

So for those of you who have reached far and distant lands,

We are still one.

We are African.

## *Body Dysphoria*

It's funny how a misunderstanding in the mind can be viewed so differently to so many people.
How a thought can become a belief,
If it's repeated enough times.
How a strong belief can navigate our words,
Our actions and our repeated behaviour.
How a repeated behaviour can become a way of life.
So when a thought is manifested and it becomes a belief,
How is that thought really seen?

If I said I could hear voices,
Would you believe me or see me as crazy?
If I said I could see things that others couldn't,
Would you call me insane or would you take heed?
If I said I believed that I was the Messiah,
Would you say I was deluded or follow me?
If I said I was fearful of things that most people aren't,
Would you say I have anxiety?
If I said I wanted to cut myself or chop off a limb,
Would you say I'm depressed or too extreme?
If I said I identified as a different race from the one I was born in,
Would I be embraced or out-casted?
If I saw health in the mirror but you saw a bag of bones,
Would you say I was anorexic or let me be?
If I said I was fat and I hated my body, but you thought I was fine,
Would you call me attention-seeking?

If I said my obesity was just thick and curvy,
Would you ridicule or champion me?

And if I thought I was in the wrong body and I believed I was a different sex,
What would you really think of me?

## *It Itches*

It itches.

It scratches.

It burns when you pee.

Now it's all red and raw.

Its covered in cottage cheese.

It feels hot when you walk.

You can't get it off your mind.

You try to act normal.

Its all going on inside.

You're over the hill.

You're down in the dumps.

You're right then you're left.

You're all paranoid.

Is that lumps?

Is that bumps?

Is it just a rash?

What is it?

## *Imperfections*

Tough hair.

Dark spots.

Keloids.

Stretch marks.

Stubbed nails.

Hairy legs.

Gapped teeth.

Fat parts.

Cellulite.

Rough scars.

Puffed lids.

Smelly farts.

Thick nose.

Sagged breast.

Clumsy.

IBS.

In-growns.

Double chin.

Rubber lips.

Bad breath.

Not bad.

Not the best.

But perfectly,

Imperfect.

## *Be Careful*

Be Careful.
Ladies, don't ever walk the streets at night.
Especially in that short, dress that's tight.
You just might cause that man to lose control.
And coerce himself into your deep, pink soul.

Be careful,
Of that Asian man with the thick, black beard
and that oversized- looking ruck sack.
He could have a bomb with him on the train
and force you to jump right on the track.

Be careful,
Put your phone away when you're walking past those hooded, black youth on the streets of London.
They could rob, chase or even stab you.
You have to be afraid of them.

Be careful,
Of that man who looks after your child.
You know the one with the prickly beard and the glint in his eyes?
Which are too close together by the way.
He might just touch her in that special place
And convince her that's how adults play.
Especially if this man is a stranger and not part of your family.
After all, family are the ones we can trust, can't we?

Be careful,
Don't you dare take a plane and fly all the way to Africa.
In that country… you'll catch HIV or even worse Ebola.
And you know those malnourished children
With the flies around their eyes?
They beg for money and put voodoo on you,
So you've got to be wise.

Be careful,
Of the ones who try to convince you of this.
They will try to instill fear and depress unification
To keep control of everything.

Divide and Conquer.
Unite and Reign.

# *My Curl is Different to Your Curl*

The kinks are woven with her-story.

The split ends show the weakness of indecision

From the withering unity.

The coils are the winds and bends taken

On the route to our destiny.

The roots run deep, holding us down in times of uncertainty.

The other strands are our friends, our family, our foes

And all the others in between.

They all play their part in our story

No matter how insignificant it may seem.

From the ones who stayed strong when we began to fray,

To the ones we cut short when they started to tear away.

They build the mass and make up the mane we have today.


And when it's not looked after, it breaks down like a nervous system

Suffering from a psychotic dis(ease).

It needs loving and nurture to heal,

The care is the hair's therapy.

Though the bush may seem wild and unmanageable,

Each strand has its weakness if stretched past its lengths.

This hair is stronger together.

When there is unity, there is always strength.

The scalp is home to the many paths
And we can choose which one we take.
The path is just as important as the journey
And all the tribulations that we face.

The oil smooths the paths which seem scary dandruff.
So I sweep the path clean of all the dust, maybes and might's
So we can face it all head on despite the tangles in our web.
Our crowns rises when our head's up
And we persevere through all the threads.

Until we reach that point when the comb runs smoothly through the kinks without a pause.
Only then, will we smile pain-free.
Only then, will we know we've got it all figured out
And we can manage it all sufficiently.
My curl is different to your curl, it's patterned differently.
The DNA; my first birthday gift.
My curl is what makes me, Me.

## *The Body is our Temple*

The body is meant to be the temple but is all too easily treated like a trash bin.

We get addicted to cosmetic surgery.

We afflict pain and adorn our skin.

We wax off and laser the unwanted.

We insert fillets and fillers to plump it.

We load our body with junk.

We then chase our next hit.

We overdose on adrenaline.

We shove in penis after penis creating cocktails of the deadliest mix.

We spray on and smooth in chemicals we can't even pronounce to change our looks which sink in through our pores.

We feed our brains with fear from the news.

We binge our eyes with gossip and negativity just for entertainment.

We share it for giggles and kicks.

We stew in other's success.

We bury our hidden desires.

We succumb ourselves to mental abuse.

We get down in the dumps and bathe in our self-pity.

We do it until we make ourselves sick.

We know it's not good but it feels good.

And then we expect our bodies to thank us for it.

## *The Heart that Beats Tirelessly*

The heart wants what the heart wants.

Even through all the aches and the pains,

The heart is stronger than any other muscle and its stamina is insane.

It beats tirelessly, working to keep you afloat.

Despite all of the abuse it endures, it's fiercely loyal.

Intelligent? I think not.

Sometimes, it beats at the wrong time when our mind tells it to stop.

Sometimes, it races when a marathon is at hand.

Sometimes, it wants to keep going when you're at your wits end.

It sends you signals and ignores the red flags,

so we end up in situations we regret.

We talk ourselves out of taking new steps,

Because the heart is constantly in battle with the head.

But the moment the heart stops doing its job,

Is the moment that we end up dead.

# ON THE SOUL

## *Trapped*

At the same time every day, my alarm rings.

But yet, I'm still tired and I don't want to answer.

I don't want to answer anymore to someone

Who wouldn't give a damn if I died tomorrow.

Someone who'd replace me like a dead battery

Just so that their circuit would continue to work.

After I'd been worked hard to the bone,

Drained even after I'm home,

Just to make ends meet and make it work for them

Whilst they make out that it's all for me.

Every day, their pockets get fatter whilst mine swell with air;

Still deficient from financial wealth and mental stimulation.

And now, the emptiness seems normal.

And the more I turn up, the more they convince me this is just how it should be.

After all, I work best when I have no drive.

I can't just get up and leave A and ride to B

When my happiness is starved and my fuel is empty

But I refuse to believe.

Is this really it?

I hit snooze on my dreams to wake up to my reality

And now I'm on pause.

My eyes stay closed as I try to hold on to my last piece of control

before I hit autopilot and replay the same routines

And fake pleasantries as I do every day.

I don't want to do this anymore.

But is the risk of the lye-in with my dreams worth the roof over my head?

It's hard to know what's best.

A life wandering where my spirits take me

Or wondering where my spirits could've taken me?

A life of hopes or a life of regret?

My alarm rings again.

My eyes roll back as I stretch back into my usual routine.

When will I finally wake up?

# *Is there a God?*

When disaster strikes, the first question is this;
Is there a God that really exist?
Desperately looking up to the skies up above;
Preaching the God that they showed taught nothing but love.
So why did we have to be cursed like this?
After doing good deeds and never taking the piss.
If the good go to heaven and the bad go to hell,
Then why are they sad when the good die as well?
They say that the good die young but they were taken too soon.
But if you believe, then weren't they lucky to be taken up quickly like
a hot-air balloon, thriving through the sky.
If you have faith, then how could you dare to even ask why?

Surely, it must have been all in the plan.
The one that was written before we were even born.
The one that has the same ending, no matter the road you explore.
If that's what you believe.

But I believe in a will that is free.
I believe in health and well-being and autonomy.
A creational being that answers before we even speak.
A being that works in synchronicity.
A being of equal value that lets us all do our part.
One that comes judgement-free and doesn't care for our past.

A creator that delivers karma even before we leave.

That only gives what we ask and gives out what we receive.

Giving every living thing a purpose for our co-existence.

Creating a ying for each yang, having the perfect balance.

A being that doesn't focus on the good and evil or the reward and punity.

But one that creates a reality based on the way how we see.

So when we see wrong, we'll receive a negative scene

But when we're seeing love, we'll get back positivity.

So when they say does God really exist, I always say yes.

Because when your energy is positive, you'll always be blessed.

# *When Will I Be Free?*

When I can travel a world without a passport,
And roam in the distant seas.
When I find land to build a home and settle,
And plant crops for me to eat.

When I can break bread with my neighbour,
Without killing anything that poos, pees or screws.
When I can wear as little or as much as I want,
in public or in private too.

When I can love myself, love others and also accept loving back.
When I don't have to spend every waking hour,
working on something for someone
that isn't joyful or stimulating at all.
When I don't have the need for money
just to keep my poor soul alive.

When I don't have to conform to group norms to be accepted in society,
And I can live my life without judgement;
Only then, will I be free.

## *Soul Mates*

I am yours. You are mine.

Even apart, our energies combine.

So in sync that it seems unreal.

Even without speaking, you know just how I feel.

Your scent is magnetic.

Your touch is electric.

Your voice is intrinsic.

Your taste is euphoric.

Your look is prolific.

Your laugh triggers mine.

Your smile is infectious.

Our chakras align.

You know just what I'm thinking.

You finish my sentence.

You know just the right spot.

You know just how I like it.

It's made just the right way.

You know exactly what to say.

And, what not to…

You cover me and I cover you.

We have the right balance.

Together,

We laugh. We cry.

We fight. We unite.

We build. We happen.

We are… Soul mates.

## *Fate*

Everything happens for a reason.
When my path crossed yours,
We both liked what we saw.
It was a match; that was sure.
So you said it was fate…
We spoke and found more.
Never seen you before
But a stride to your door?
So you said it was fate.

Then you rain-checked our first date.
A big no-no for me.
Then you pleaded your plea.
"Don't give up on me."
"You don't know where this could go."
"Just give us a chance," you said.
And I said, "Okay."
So you said it was fate…

Was it fate that I felt just as lonely as you?
Was it fate that you sought company online too?
Was it fate you saw me and I also saw you?
Was it fate you said yes when I also swiped right?
Was it fate that you wouldn't give up without a fight?
Was it fate that we met up,
Shared our first kiss and stayed out all night?

Were our souls drawn to each other like magnets attract?
Were things set up on purpose so we'd interact?
Was it written in the stars that your mother birthed you in the same year as mine?
Or that our parents would both live south of the line?
Or that our star signs would just seamlessly intertwine?

Or was it just right place, right time?
A coincidence.

## *Is the Grass Greener?*

From where I stand on the grass,
It's all patchy and dark
And the leaves have a golden hue.
Like they are slowly dying from dehydration.
They look rough from frustration
Of being trodden on for too long
Without love and care taken into consideration,
And my heart weeps for the unconscious abuse.

I long to look for the grass that's long, luscious and green
And smiles from the inside out.
And looking out to the distance, it's so easily found.
It's the grass I've been thinking about.

As I search for the perfect spot,
The grass looks grey,
So I keep searching for what I once saw in the distance.
But it seems so hard to find.

And when I look back to where I came from,
That grass looks greener than I remembered
And certainly greener than where I now reside.
So I have to stop and think.
And really ask myself,
Is the grass actually greener on the other side?

## *Plants Have Feelings Too*

Why is it that when we see a flower, we pick it because it's pretty?
The moment it's picked, it slowly dies and for what? Our vanity?
Imagine someone spotting your beautiful face
And plucking it straight from your neck?
That is literally the equivalent of what a giant could do to us
But as humans, we take advantage.

Yes, fruits and vegetables are for eating and they keep us energised.
But why pick a plant just to pick it?
Why chop a tree trunk just to chop it?
It's their oxygen that gives us life.
We all have a purpose on this earth,
And sometimes, we forget to empathise.
All we think about is our selfish needs,
And get caught up within our own lives.

Just because you can't see it, it doesn't mean it's not happening.
Just because you can't hear it, it doesn't mean plants don't cry, weep or mourn.
Just because you can't feel it, it doesn't mean it doesn't hurt.
Just remember, plants have feelings too.

## *Mirror, Mirror*

The worst time to look in the mirror is in the morning,
Because that's when I see the real me.
I see the crust built up from keeping my eyes shut.
I see the trail of dribble that's left my lips
from a night of dream chasing.
Dark marks embedded under layers of skin,
That remind me of all the mistakes that I made.

Through my eyes, I see all of the hidden secrets
that I prefer to keep locked away.
I see all of the let down's and setbacks
that knock a chip of hope off my positive outlook.
And my mind remembers the comments I'd rather forget,
But they're engrained in my memory.
I see the lost, little girl still trying to find her way
Though she has no clue if she's heading in the right direction.

I see the fresh start that comes with the breaking dawn
As the water splashes against my face.
The towel wipes the slate clean and dry
in an attempt to strengthen the grip at the base.
A pale ghost of imperfections looks back
As my dark eyes are relentlessly read.
I paint on the make up to mask it all and look flawless
So I can face the day ahead.

## *Those Streets*

Whenever I pass by those streets, it always brings me back in time.
To the days of sausage and skirt rolls before school.
Bacon butties, chips with a touch of brown sauce.
To the days of five day passes and falling asleep on the line,
When his breath soothed my sleep as it tingled down my spine.

To the days when shoobs were free;
To willy bounce and dutty whine.
When the party's gossip would spread through the town
Like wild fire.
To the days of £3 cinema tickets
With McD's vouchers on the back.
To the days of gold rings and multiple ear piercings
And stopping by Ken when we needed new bling.

To the days of G.A.T on Ontop FM
And feeling on top of the world when you knew one of them.
Geoffrey Chaucer boys fighting you for your attention
Or feeling you when they were feeling you
Or your friend, not to mention.

To the days of knocking for my friends without making a call
'cos that was cool back then.
We didn't plan in advance.
We'd go where those streets took us and still have a laugh.

Even when our mothers were expecting us home,

Worried sick to their stomach with their eyes wide open,

Whilst the blind led the blind; we thought we knew it all.


To the days of consistently bumping in to someone that you knew with someone new;

And changing your route just to follow them too.

To the days of girl gangs and rolling in batches of 5.

It always felt odd but I couldn't quite figure out why.


Girls on the bus, giving you the cold eye,

So only making contact for a limited time.

Those same girls that would batter you on the top of the 36 bus and then steal your gold chain.

Punches that rung so hard, you could hear your mother's voice in your ear;

If you don't hear, you will feel;

As though she prophesised it from the start.


I used to roam those streets in uniform

With my friends still in their uniform, taking the long way home.

Those streets weren't my streets but they felt like my own.

Southampton Way was my link to those streets.

Linking up with my links and connecting dots with my feet.

Walking the dog, Marbles and making new friends;

That's just how it worked in those days, in the ends.

I used to ride in those streets and get backies on bikes.

Riding home with the boys in the middle of the night.

From North Peckham to Crane Block to Lettsom to South.

Wherever those streets led, those wheels were about.

From Chinese to chicken shops all on the front line

Where the yardies stood like soldiers all day and all night.

Those streets led back to Blue Park and Green Park

Where we chilled after dark.

And that bridge that's locked off,

Where that kiss stole my heart.

Those streets always protected me like the big brother I never had.

They watched from every street corner

And lit the way like tall street lamps.

Those streets made me wise and peeled my eyes wide open.

So now I look both ways before I cross and then choose a focus.

Now when I pass by those streets, so much has changed.

New people, new shops; gentrifying the lot.

Now owning those streets feels like a distant memory.

Did I leave or get pushed out of the localities?

Was the violence too much? Was I all partied out?

Did maturity take its toll? Or was I told to get out? Just like Chris.

When they came, they cleared up all the urban myths.

They smoothed the bumps on the road and covered up all the rifts.

Though I've moved on and moved out, it is still clear to see.

I left a part of me in those streets and they'll always be part of me.

## *Coleby Path*

Peeping out of my window, looking down at them on the path,
Longing to fit in like the missing piece in the puzzle.
It's ironic because now, it just doesn't make sense.
I longed to lower my standards and mask my intelligence just to be like them.

The loud mouths on the block.
Those mouths that opened wide to air their dirty laundry.
Those mouths that jeered the other,
As the pizza delivery scooter "disappeared."
Those mouths that outraged in uproar from the pound that wasn't quite up to the wall.
Those mouths that spat bars onto the path
Whilst the instrumental drove them all mental.
I used to long to join in with the fun and games.

And now when I see those loud mouths on the path,
It no longer seems quite the same.
Their jaws have all sunken and gone all concave.
Yet, they're still planted in the path just like stubborn weeds.
Soaking up the same atmosphere and inhaling the toxicity
From the same weeds which blackened their spirit,
Sucked their life and slowed their footsteps;
It's no wonder they're stuck.

But just like a matured, wishing dandelion,

I've blossomed and gone with the wind.

Dispersing seeds to plant and germinate in new places.

And they're still stuck.

Trapped in the pavement on the path.

Like the puzzle piece forced into the wrong part.

They're still stuck.

And it's hard not to look down at them from my silver-lined cloud

As the wind swiftly blows me right past.

## *Don't Worry Little Girl*

You are more than the names they call you.
In fact, it's those names that drive you to be the exact opposite.
You don't have to be liked. And you most certainly don't have to like them.
If they don't like it, they'll lump it and that door will open up for some one new to replace them.
You don't need to impress your friends just to be popular.
For if they have a genuine interest in you, then they'll stick around.

You don't have to compete in any and everything.
You don't need to prove points about your ability.
As long as you know the score, you'll silently win.
You don't have to keep up, everybody's path is different.
What's right for Sally may not be right for Susie.
And what Sally thought was right may not have been right at all.

You don't have be the loudest one in the room to be noticed and you don't have to fill the gaps of silence.
You have a whirlwind of thoughts and there is power in your words, when you speak even just a sentence.
Not everyone will like your alternative thoughts and not everyone can handle it.
Not everybody will understand you but those who care will take the time to peel back the layers of your skin.

In life, you'll have to understand that only when you're older,
Some misunderstandings will then make sense.
Some people have their own battles and demons they're fighting so their actions just won't make any sense.
Until you unpick it and understand that their reality is different from yours and you'll never be able to change that.
Don't worry little girl, if things get too much, you can always take a step back.

Worrying won't change the outcome, so don't worry little girl; for that is time wasted.
Why wait for the worst if you've done your best?
If it can't change, then, don't worry about it.

# *A Blessing and a Curse*

The depth of the soul comes as both a blessing and a curse.
It's precious like the hidden diamond buried deep into the earth.
So a special kind of torch is needed to guide us through the dark.
To navigate through the walls of disappointment
and relight the once lost spark.
A hard hat is needed for if you get lost along the way;
Listening to the doubting voices that can lead you astray.
Those voices that drag you under and try to bury you deep.
Lost under the stones and rubble from a fearful memory.

Be Warned:
The soul is home to the hurt that's been lying dormant for centuries.
But it's also the place where our true inner desires can be found
And then released.
It's where life's regrets and wishes reside.

If you go deep enough,
You may see what you'd rather not find.
But you might see something amazing
that you didn't even know that you had inside.
Because sometimes the most precious of gems are created
under very immense pressure.

## *You are What You Eat*

The skin is said to replace itself every 28 days
And rebuild off the food that we eat.
So although some don't take it literally,
You literally are everything that you eat.

Now that doesn't mean that if you eat beef,
You'll be mooing and grazing all day
But it does mean that when you eat foods that are high in fat,
The result is ultimately that.

And when you eat fruits that are full of colour,
You become filled with life and vitality.
And I certainly don't want to be fake, fast, fat, cheap
Or even easy.

So I make sure that I feast on alkaline water
To purify and balance my soul.
And absorb the natural sunlight
To accentuate my internal glow.

I digest motivational talks
From people doing better than me.
And take in the people around me
And take note of their positivity.

I inhale the fresh air slowly
In times of uncertainty.
I make a meal of my emotions
So that I can guide them directly.

And then, I taste the fruits of my labour
From building a better me.
So when your body is fed food that's poison,
It's no wonder you come up in rashes, eczema, acne, high blood pressure, diabetes
And dare I say it, cancer.

And when your life is filled with pessimism and low spirits,
It's no wonder you suffer depression.
Your body feeds off what you give it
And also what you expose it to.
So be careful what you eat
Because you are what you consume.

## *Negative Energy*

You drain me.

You're like a blood sucking leech extracting my soul,

Depleting my energy and leaving me lifeless.

And after you leave, I need a recharge.

Your words are destructive and destroy everything in its path.

You can't see the bright side,

You can't even laugh.

Your eyes only breathe fire.

Your outlook is bleak.

You find the bad in the good.

Your mindset is weak.

But having said that, is it just mine?

Your strength is so strong, I need a lifeline.

Is your gloom overpowering?

Or is my hope not enough?

Though I'm not sure, being with you is tough.


I just want to plug you in sometimes,

Until you're 100 percent,

No matter how hard I try to fight,

It's never time well spent.

It is a burden for me to spend time with you.

I try avoiding you at all costs.

I just wish you could see the silver lining sometimes,

But for me, your soul is lost.

# $E=MC^2$

For every action there is an equal and opposite reaction;
The simple physics of life.
For every action there is a consequence.
So, when you push me, I could drop to the ground with just as much power.
Or I could push back with just as much force.
When you lie, I could believe you with just as much faith.
Or I could lie back with just as much deceit.
When you cheat, I could forgive you with just as much heart.
Or I could cheat back with just as much treachery.
When you take, I could give, with generous open arms.
Or I could take back, with just as much conceit.

When you give, I could take, with just as much greed.
Or I could give back with just as much love.
When you argue, I could argue back with just as much aggression.
Or I could simmer it down with just as much silence.
When you cry, I could cry back with just as much tears.
Or I could give you a reason to laugh with just as much jokes.
If you fall from a cliff, you could drop with just as much speed.
Or you could float, fly or soar with just as much glide.
For every action there is a consequence; a consequence that you can choose.
For every consequence, there leaves a mark.
And the only person held accountable,
Is you.

## *Why Can't We Live In Simplicity?*

Why can't we live in simplicity?

Why can't we run around and be free?

Why can't we wear simple cloths to cover our decency?

Why can't we build our own homes for our loved ones and family?

Why can't we plant our own foods and cook them without spending a penny?

Why can't we be happy for others without feeling jealousy?

Why can't we enjoy the moment without snapping it instantly?

Why do we allow ourselves to be consumed by this mentality?

Why can't we live in simplicity?

## *When I Die*

I don't need a religious service or readings from a book.
I don't need hymns.
If you want, you can sing and you can wear whatever you choose.
I don't need a horse or a carriage.
I don't need expensive limousines.
I don't need tall hats or you dressed up in black.
I don't even need a casket.

Just bury me straight into the ground.
Where my body can disintegrate and give back to the wondrous giving earth.
Don't give me flowers, give me seeds.
So my minerals can flourish other's needs.
Creating plants and trees just so you can breathe.
Let my energy be recycled while the Sun does its work.
After all, we're all here to nourish this earth.

My soul can rest 'till it finds another host if it wants.
But you don't need to mourn my death.
Celebrate my life with parties and eulogies.
Though tears may be shed, make them tears of joy,
As I have finally done my part.
Though life should be lived and fully enjoyed,
Death completes the circle of life.

## *Reset*

If only life came with a reset button,
Then, we could start all over again.
Removing all bugs and viruses we caught on the way,
And refreshing our system again.

If there was ever an error that caused us to freeze,
We'd hit a button to undo the problem.
We'd lose all of the changes that we didn't save,
But we'd have a way of solving the problem.

When we got hurt unexpectedly,
We could just rub out all the pain and the grief.
We could simply erase our wrong-doings from our story of life,
By turning over a new leaf.

If we didn't like where something was going,
We could stop at that point and repeat it all from the start.
Changing our input to change the outcome,
And create a whole new path.

What a life it would be if we could stop and repeat,
At any given point in time.
Being so caught up on making it right,
That we never reach the finish line.

## *There are Two Types of People*

In this world, there are two types of people;
Ones who make excuses,
And ones that demand that obstacles are excused out of their way.

Ones who never believed that it was possible,
And ones the doing it, who created the space.

Ones who accept that some things are "just meant to be,"
And ones that will go out and get what they need.

Ones who will tell you a story for why 'it is what it is,'
And ones that will tell you a story of how they did it.

Ones who preach that good things come to those who wait,
And ones who know good things come quicker when you go out and get it.

There are two types of people, in this world;
"The 99" and "The Top 1 percent."
Which one are you?

## *Re-birth*

At 25, I was born again.
It was like for the first time I could see.


I learnt to walk without any body holding my hand.
I learnt to read energy and remove myself from the bad.
I learnt how to write and channel my thoughts and emotions
I learnt to speak my mind and "No," quickly became one of my favourite words.
I learnt how to say "No," to lowering my standards and spending time with people who wanted me to.


I learnt that it was okay that everybody didn't like and accept me for me.
And I made new friends who had the same interests as me.
I didn't need to throw any tantrums, cry,
Chuck my toys, question why.
Not once, did I need to make a fuss.
Because, I learnt how to appropriately express myself
And self-expression is a must.

# ON SEX & RELATIONSHIPS

# *First Love*

Everything is new. Everything is fresh.
Everything is love. You can't be without them.
Every time they ring your phone, every time you get a text,
Your heart springs into action, ready for the next step.

Their embrace sparks you off and their eyes transport you
to a whole new universe.
You share your first kiss on the bridge whilst no one else is there,
Which you can't get enough of, so you take it to the stairs,
In that estate where the door opens, if you pull hard enough.
You sit for hours and just kiss because you don't want that moment
to pass.

Until you progress and make love for the first time,
When it just slips in without thinking and it feels so right.
The sex is like no other because the connection is rare.
Even a quickie feels like the world is on pause.

Until you almost get caught.
What would his mum have thought?
Over to study but that Jamo was under my son;
And it would've been only him that caught the tan from his mum;
And we couldn't have had that.
You love their family and friends
And you know they all love you back.

Their words soothe your mind

And their breathing becomes meditation while you sleep.

Even when you're not together.

The alarm of his voice wakes you up,

Whilst the heat of the phone burns through your ear.

And the crust forms from the dribble left

From a young one struck.

And even when things go sour,

You still hold on because you're stuck.

And even though you want your happy ending to happen at all costs,

Nothing hurts more than a first love lost.

# *Heartbreak*

High expectations was the cause of my heartbreak.

I thought you'd never disappoint but you did and now it aches.

Lies told from the pedestal that I'd put you on.

Games played in revenge. Games I didn't find fun.

Playing me like a fiddle while I danced to every word.

Turning hot and then cold, but keeping me warm,

In the hope that I'd be served.

But you dished me up a stone-cold plate of reality

That slapped me in my face.

Forced me to move on, though my heart stayed with you for years,

Hoping it would catch up with me one day.

And it did, when you came back into my life.

I thought it would work.

I thought things were different

But they turned out to be the same.

Fool me once, shame on you.

Fool me twice, shame on me.

Does the pain ever fade?

Or is it just masked until the memory of the past is triggered

Like the bullets in a gun.

Decades gone. New relationships.
I still think about you until this day.
Wondering if it would have ever worked
And whether this pain will go away.
We've both travelled down our new paths;
Which live in parallel but rarely cross
On the poetic roads that we take.
But nothing or no one can replace you in my heart.

Your memory still lives in the cracks
of my original heartbreak.

## *Love Bites*

Love licks.

Love tastes.

Love clutches on to your skin.

Love tickles your soft spot.

Love laps you again.

Love strokes you over and over.

Love takes the breath from your lungs.

Love makes your eyes water.

Love stands hairs on end.

Love rushes blood to your head.

Love heats you up.

Love turns you cold.

Love is red but love is blue.

Love savours you deeply

Love bruises your vessels.

Love leaves a red mark.

Love turns purple and black.

Love fights. Love hugs.

Love kisses. Love sucks.

Love fades.

Love bites.

## *Life Partner*

You get me.

Or at least you try to.

And when a misunderstanding arises,

Together, we figure us out.

You make things right.

Or at least you try to.

And when help is needed or wanted,

Without fail, the other is there.

You have seen the high and the lows,

The laughter and the frowns,

The wellness and the illness,

The wealth and the grind,

And yet you're still here.

Holding me down while I lift you up.

We are a team.

Just us two.

You are my weakness and I am your strength.

And we're even stronger together.

Where one lacks, the other one thrives;

Balancing us out.

We're not perfect.

But it works.

And I wouldn't have it any other way.

## *Under the Rug*

In the grand house at the end of the street, lives a beautiful rug.
It's adorned with patterns and whirls and twirls.
And when others are captured, the owners stand proud, showcasing their works.
But no one knows what lies underneath.
Underneath, there's a whole new world.

Under the rug lives;
The cobwebs from an under-used hug.
The crawling ants from their wandering thoughts.
The dried tears from a sunken soul.
The purple bruises from a punching bag.
The lost voice from a tiring box.
The forgotten plug to light up their life.
The on-switch to the listening ear.
The granted they'd taken time and time again.
The years-old cereal liar that slipped out of the bowl.
The dirty pair of underwear from an un-invited guest.
The stain from a bleeding heart that was constantly on the mend.
The spilt secrets they couldn't find out.

But as the people passed by, they always stopped to admire
the wondrous aesthetics of the rug.

It's lasted so long.

It looks absolutely stunning.

It simply lights up the room.

But they have no idea of what lies underneath,

Even when it bursts through the seams.

It's all kept so quiet and snug.

The cracks. The cockroaches.

The dust. The mites.

The nuts. The screws.

The crumbs. The empty packet of crisps.

That deep, black hole.

They haven't a clue.

But it's fine because

It's all swept under the rug.

## *It Hurts*

We kiss.

We touch, but I'm vacant behind.

I know what you want, but that's not on my mind.

Your hands are so eager. I just wished you'd slow down.

And though my face fakes a smile, my hearts in a frown.

Handling me like your steak; like an unruly child.

But I'm not ready to eat, and done nothing too wild.

But you can't see that.

There's no rush. I'm not going anywhere.

But your hands are still keen to take it there.

Your elbows,

Your knees, all in the wrong place.

*Ouch.* I smile and tears weep inside.


I give up.

Just take me.

I lay on my back.

*Scrape. Scratch. Scrape.*

It's in.

My eyes reach back.

My walls rub raw and my eyes glaze clear.

But it's okay, 'cos it'll be over soon.

And we'll both be happy.

And that's how it works.


But no one knows just how much it hurts.

## *Is This Really What I Want?*

A life of mediocre.

A life of just getting by.

Vanilla sex and flavourless conversations.

Over-explaining myself so that you can understand.

Routine Spontaneity.

Watching you watch TV.

Sharing memes and basic jokes.

Making each other tea.

Before we spill it with riveting questions like,

"How was your day?"

Hearing the same stories.

Acting as if it were the first.

Taking into account you don't quite get it.

Finding escapism while you sleep.

Only to withdraw when you awake.

And crawl into our morning routine.

Is this really what I want?

I will never know,

'Cos I'm not willing to take the chance to find out and let go.

## *I just want the D*

A man could offer me flowers,

B as flashy as a light,

C me home in the night,

Eat with me at the finest restaurants,

F with my mum, my daddy and my sister too,

Give me all the latest designers,

Hate hanging with his friends and have a fancy car but

I don't care about all that.

Just give me what I need.

Kut all the bullshit.

Let's get straight to it.

My mind has been craving for it.

N now I want it.

Over the couch, over the bed and the kitchen spread.

Please don't make me beg.

Quit twiddling with your thumbs.

R you ready or not? Let's

See if you're ready to show me what you've got.

Time is of the essence.

U know that as well. I've been

Very patient and your

X will never ever compare so

Y are you playing around?

Zere's only one thing that's missing from inside of me.

And it's just what I want and that is the D!

## *The one*

You are the one for me;

Right now.

You fit into my situation perfectly.

I don't need to change much and things flow so we're good.

Not much about you bothers me.

So I'll stick with you until things dry up,

Or until things get too sticky.

And then I'll find another one that seems…

Just right

For me.

## *Sixty-nine*

I'll be the six if you be the nine.
I'll be the best six you've ever had.
One time is enough
But it takes two to tango.
I'll make you three's whilst on my knees.
I'll put the spring back in your step.
Just like when you were young.
So feel three and let the four play.
Tasting so good, you'll have to lick all five.

I'll be the best six you've ever had.
I would've taken you to seventh heaven by the time you eight me.
I'll leave you on cloud nine.
We'll both come at the same time.
I'll grab yours if you grab mine.
I'll ride 'till you bus.
I'll sit on your face.
I'll hoover up like a cleaner,
So let us both slot into place.

Just like the days of tops and tails, where the spoons intertwine.
I'll be the six if you be the nine.

# *Will I ever be Good Enough?*

My face is too round.

My farts are too loud.

My acne's too black.

My stomach's too fat.

My pussy's too wack.

My lips are too cracked.

My hair is too bushy.

In the morning, it's rough.

My teeth are too yellow,

I don't brush them enough.

And to top it off, my snacks are too much.

And now every time I put the fork to my mouth,

All I can think of is you.

The list of forbidden foods are endless, just to keep you.

And now, if I slip and divulge, it's never with you.

Working hard to change me, but mostly for you.

And though changes are there, there's so much more to do.

But the question is, will I ever be good enough?

## *You Cheated on Me*

You lied.

You broke my trust.

You cheated on me.

You made the tears stream.

You made my heart weep.

You made me nauseous.

You made me paranoid.

Questions constantly on my mind.

Where were you?

Who were you with?

Why are you smiling?

What's made you happy?

Will you do it again?

You've done it before,

So it's hard to know.

And it lingers in my head.

I told you I forgave,

But I knew I couldn't forget.

But it's fine,

Because we all have skeletons in the back of our closet.

# *My Sweet Valentine*

They say the way to a man's heart is through his stomach
But that's clearly the way to mine.
It's been years and you're still my valentine.
It didn't take long for you to make my heart bounce once
Then twice.
Though the ride hasn't been a walk in the park,
We still smile through.
We got comfortable and now I adore you.
I'd jump through hoops and climb the steepest mountains
Just to be with you.
A hole in one for our first Valentines, what a result.
We did Black Panther. And you've cooked to which I can't pick no fault.

Here's to team us.
Here's to summer lovin' that took us to new heights.
Here's to first trips abroad.
Here's to a future so bright.

Caught that five star intercontinental love.
I caught both feelings and flights;
That unforgettable love.
Our love is locked and our bond is unbreakable.

We are one.

You are the beat to my drum.

You are my midnight summer's dream.

You are my summer fun.

You are my best friend.

We ride till we die.

Through thick and thin.

In sickness and in health.

We will always fight through like the champions we are.

Where there's a will, there is a way; there is a way through the storms.

The past years have been fab. Here's to many more.

## *Best Friends*

The day we first met, I never thought we'd end up like this.
Your whole demeanour was reserved and I wasn't used to it.
Your words ran away from you on the phone
So they were lost when we would meet.
There's usually power in silence but it freaked me out
when you were meek.

When we began, you were awkward, you were like a closed book.
I used to long to finger your pages but you would never let me look.
The front page was so attractive; tall, thick handsome
With deep, dark eyes.
Book sleeves covered in fine cloths; the synopsis intrigued my mind.
Though the seals were locked tight,
I was still determined to discover what was inside.

They say never judge a book by its cover and now I know why.
Because as the hairs have begun to sprout from dear father time's ears,
I've seen your kinks. I've seen your cracks.
I've seen your scars. I've seen your tears.
Those tears that fell into the tissue when I made your heart bleed.
And we bled and shed together as we cut each other deep.
It's that same tissue which worked to heal our wounds
And seal us back together.
And now our bond is unbreakable; our bond is stronger than ever.

## ~ 117 ~

I could never really tell whether it was me
Or my friends that have distanced,
But now it feels like you're all that I have.
Bald patches where they shed like weak hairs over the years.
Leaving only grey scale movies that creep between the gaps.

A wise person once said, "Never make a man your everything because when he leaves, you'll have nothing."
And somehow, I've managed to do just that.
You're my shoulder to cry on; my rock to lean on;
My partner in crime and my best memories are in colour with you.

Before you, I wandered aimlessly in the deep, dark woods.
I couldn't find what I was looking for, but I knew that I would.
Then I stumbled across your door, though at first you wasn't there,
I crept inside and explored; then fell asleep on your bed.
That bed that became home to all the laughs and all the dread.
To all the squeaks, creaks, rough, tumble and bends.
But it's those ups, downs, those memories that've made us best friends.

Because when it's all said and done, at the end of the day,
I have you to hold me tight.
Protective arms like Papa Bear's that keep me warm in the night,
Though sometimes it's too hot,
It's too heavy and it's hard, and airtight.
For me, it is perfect.
For me, it's just right.

## Those Hands

What a pair.

Large enough to grab a load,

But, tender enough to let me know you care.

The sight alone of the thickness takes my imagination there.

A span so wide, it reaches the corners of the earth.

Digits so thick, it competes with your girth.

Like a sixth sense, I can feel it.

Without speaking, you let me know that you can handle it.

Trails of melanin run deep through the veins of your palms,

So I know that you have heart.

They say heart is where the home is, so where you fly, I'll land.

And I know you'll catch me when I fall for you.

Your tender back strokes leave tribal marks,

Like Ashanti, I'll be foolish for you.

Palms of authority. Spank my behind.

Take me back to school and teach me a lesson.

Then soothe it like a boo boo and I'll never regret it.

I'm love struck by those hands.

What a lovely pair.

Large enough to grab a load,

But, tender enough to let me know you care.

## *Vitamin S*

Most days, she is good, so she just gets on with things.
And honestly won't bother you at all.
But there are times in the month when she craves that connection,
She craves that touch. She craves that stroke. She craves that kiss.
And if she doesn't get it, that's when the beast comes out, hunting for its next hit.
She will worm all over you, in search of her next feed
And coerce your feeding time to sync with hers.
Her body is bare and she demands that yours is too.
As she works her claws through your buttons.
Her strongest sense is her taste, so she uses her tongue,
As she explores through your fairground.
Your head in her hands. Her arms are locked straight until your mind is refuelled
With knowledge right from her divine source of energy.
You'll soak up every last bit and she makes sure of it
All before you use your battery.
Her legs lock around you whilst you do your work.
Her hips crave for that 100 per cent.

She doesn't let go until your battery is drained,
And she is charged with horse power that's built to last.
When you collapse, the beast retreats back into her shell
For another fortnight or two.
And you are left to do what you do best,
Whilst she does what she needs to do.

## *Smooth like Butter*

Look at those lips.

Smooth like butter. Firm like cherry skin.

Lips that bounce off mine like castles whilst my heart does back flips.

Lips that mesmerise eyes with moves that are hypnotic,

And I'm drunk off the concoction.

Soaked in sexual chocolate.

Dazed by delicious sin.

Just like a measuring tape, those lips don't miss an inch.

And after a dozen, I've grown a foot despite my curled over toes.


Lips that appreciate nip slips,

Like a playground does ice-cream cones.

Lips that breathe so many sweet nothings, I need to see a dentist.

Leaving my mouth wide open

And you've only just scratched the surface.

Nibbling on me like a rabbit with a fresh carrot stick.

Nibbling on me like a secret eater who's meant to be on a diet.

Because it always tastes better when you're not meant to have it.


Smiling like that cat who got the cream

When you've only licked the tip.

Like an Iceberg in global warming, I anticipate the change in climax.

And the eruption of the earthquake does not bother me one bit.

Oohh… and I can feel the bounce of your lips around it.

Smooth like butter. Firm like cherry skin.

Fiending like a crack addict searching for their next hit.

## *Give me knowledge*

Take me school, college and university.
Take me on a trip around the world.
Show me your geography of my anatomy.
Teach me things that I haven't explored.
I need that times table knowledge
Those factors that make multiple climbs at the wall.

Teach me my A.B.C's until I'm sick to D.E.F
Of you on my G-spot you so easily find.
I need that jaw-dropping knowledge with the Oh's and the Ah's
As you take me by surprise.

That knowledge that makes my eyes roll back,
Searching for why I didn't already have you in my life.
Stroke me with that light bulb knowledge
That leaves me numb and dumbfounded
As my soul begins to rise.

I want your head in my hands.
Your play on words between my thighs.
If you give me all you've got, I'll open up my vulnerable side.
Let your aural work blow my mind.
I want you to leave me saturated with wisdom but thirsty for more.
That's the type of knowledge I need to find.

# *A Royal Flush*

Nipples fiddled between his fingers.

Tongues slathering and leaving snail trails.

Traces of tingles standing hairs to attention.

Lungs expanding at the feel of warm breath.

Worshipping each other in our birthday suits.

Call it a royal flush of hearts.


He bows down at the sight of my throne.

My jewel is given the royal treatment.

Whilst my tongue works its magic.

My heart is already pouncing and his palms are already sweating.

His penis teases and then it slips in.

And it drives me up the wall.

Hands climbing as he delves in deeper

Like a submarine into the ocean.

Waves of passion rise then crash like a brewing tsunami underneath my skin.


The lust balloons as my back is blown in.

Kisses between strokes. Eyes glazed over in joy.

A pulse of pleasure as he pounds.

My jaw drops in astoundment.

As he digs like a spade in the sand, crashing into my castle.

As my flood gates overflow and open wide.

Call it a royal flush of hearts

Love me.

Love me.

Love me.

Splash.

## *Relationship Goals*

When they see them kiss and cuddle all over their feed,
They say that's relationship goals.
They see the cute messages, the laughs, the pet names
And the goofy handshakes.
They see the dates and the gifts when the boy did good
And she said "yes,"
They see the trips, the wedding pics, the boomerangs and the gifs,
So they say that's relationship goals.

But when the camera's switched off,
No one knows what happens behind closed doors.
No one sees the struggle or the come up
From the times when they were poor.
No one sees the fights and the lies and the tears and deceit.
No one knows the amount of times she's had to put up with the sheet.
No one sees the time he forgot and couldn't be bothered with it.
No one knows about that baby and whether it's really his.

They see the filter but can't see through the rose-tinted specs.
We see the highlights whilst they hide in lowlight
To cover up all their mess.
They say seeing is believing, but we see the best ten secs.
We only see the tip of the iceberg whilst the water drowns the rest.

So why should that be my relationship goal

When the picture's off-target?

How can I believe in a story that doesn't really exist?

I want us both on the same page.

We'll both pick up the slack.

I want someone reliable

So we can have each other's back.

I want that mutual understanding

So we can build on the trust.

I want that know us but not about us.

I want that real kind of love.

Where we disagree in private

And never issue public apologies.

Where our best memories are in our head

And not on our news feed.

And when times get tough,

We stick together to work through it.

A best friend and family.

A real-ationship.

# ON FAMILY & FRIENDS

# *A Peacock in the Jungle*

She blossomed before the rest
And her beauty was noticeable.
She stood out like a beautiful peacock
Walking through the jungle.
So she pranced and strut with confidence
And the creatures admired her looks.
But the wild cats saw her as a threat
And they stalked every step that she took.

They watched as the feathers glowed in the light
And they began to lick their lips.
The peacock barely took any notice
relishing in all the changes.
They surrounded her like hyenas in the jungle,
In search for their next prey.
And she felt their presence, as the whispering started
And the sneering hissed in her ear;
Like snakes.
Goading and mocking the feathers
Until she eventually caved.
And felt ashamed of her blossoming features,
because they still all looked the same.

Tears soaked her cheeks as the hyena's laughed hysterically

at how she'd began to change.

And her voice was silenced,

as they all drowned her out,

So in plain sight is where she hid.

Trying to blend in with all the hyenas,

until all the taunting had stopped.

They made her feel small for being bright and colourful,

so ever since then,

She never tried to stand out or be different

from anyone else again.

# *A Friend for each Finger*

When I was 17,

Someone once told me that they could count all their good friends on one hand.

But I didn't understand;

Because I had so many.

But now, I know,

Because I can do the same.

And three of my friends are family.

## *Sleepovers*

Where will I stay this weekend?
What party will we go to?
Who will we prank?
What guys will we cry over?
What movies will we watch?
What food will we eat?
Who'll sleep heads or tails?

Are they coming to crash?
Will we play truth or dare?
Will we stay up all night?
When will we knock out?
Who knows?
But one thing's for sure,
I'm definitely not
Staying at home.

## *Shoobs*

It's been planned all week.

But we don't know whose it is.

We just know we are going.

And we know where it is.

It's the word on the street.

So everybody is gassed.

The moon is alive.

We are all dressed up.

We turn up at the block.

We see the loud crowd.

The usual's and the new.

My face creeps a smile.

Will we get in? Will we not?

We climb up the stairs.

We're finally here.

The doorbell rings.

The door opens.

I can't see a thing.

But we walk inside.

The music pulsates.

Everyone is dancing.

So I wind my waist.

My friends make a circle.

And he creeps behind.

His crutch on my ass.

His hands on my waist.

Gyrate. Gyrate.

Gyrate. Gyrate.

No alcohol. No Drugs.

We're all high on life.

The music gets wild and so does the crowd.

Rocking and knocking the house in the block.

Who does it belong to?

No one has a clue.

'Till they hear a loud smash.

The music cuts off.

The lights turn on.

We all look around.

She's in a headscarf.

She's shouting us out.

It's officially been locked.

Shoobs.

## *Jealousy*

Wolves dressed in sheep's clothing, trying to befriend me.

Drawn to my warmth, my opinions and intellectuality.

Giving time, giving love, giving energy.

Learning what they can to use it against me.

Throwing digs when they can, due to their insecurities.

Because the best friend of Misery is Company.

If they're not, then they can't stand when you're happy.

This is hate.

This is green eye.

This is jealousy.

## *Were you there?*

I remember you were there when you wanted to go out,
But were you there when I wanted to try something new?
I remember you were there on that shopping spree.
But were you there when I needed that £10?

I remember you were there when you invited me out,
But were you there when it was time to pay the bill?
I remember you were there on those late night drives,
But were you there when I needed a drive home?
I remember you were there at the birthday parties,
But were you there to help me clean up?

I remember you where there when we broke up,
But were you there on those lonely nights?
I remember you were there at the sleepovers,
But were you there the nights that I couldn't get to sleep?

I remember you were there to gossip all night on the phone,
But were you there when they gossiped about me?
I remember you were there that time when everyone was,
But were you there when they all turned their back?

I remember you were there when no one else was,
But were you there when you had company?
I remember you were there when you needed a friend,
But were you there when I needed one back?

**BEHIND THOSE DARK EYES** | *On Family & Friends*

## *True Friends*

True friends are the family you choose.

You'll share the best jokes and are always in sync.

They never judge you and if they do, you don't care.

They are loyal beyond measure and are always there;

Even when they don't want to be.

They'll follow you, while you fulfil your wildest dreams.

And if they can't, they'll let you travel the world and be there when you're back.

They accept all the changes;

Even the ones they disagree with.

They'll help you make the wrong right again.

And even though they'll pick you up when you are down,

They're always there to serve you up a plate of cold, hard, honest truth.

True friends are the family you choose.

## *Fake friends*

They listen to all your secrets.
They promise they won't tell.
They scorn at your successes.
They want you to do well,

But not better than them.

They keep a close eye on your lover.
They're quick to notice their mistakes.
They're quick to talk when you're not there.
They laugh at your downfall.

They do what everyone else is doing.
They always show up late.
They can't make it to that event.
They forget to call you back.

But they always need your advice.

They're down for the fun times.
They up and leave you in the lurch.
They call you when they're scared.
When you give, they always take.
They're only with you when it's convenient
'Cos the truth is, they're fake.

**BEHIND THOSE DARK EYES** | *On Family & Friends*

## *Betrayal*

I thought you were going to be there for me.

You knew how I felt because it was plain to see.

You were there for the highs, the lows and the reality.

But you still decided to deceive me.

So much choice but mine looked better it seems clearly.

Sometimes your best friends can be your worst enemy.

You wanted what I had so you lied. You hid.

You betrayed me.

## *When friends become family*

You don't need to impress.
You know who I am.
You know the girl behind the make-up.
You know my bare skin.
Even when I hide it, you see through the rigmarole.
Our eyes are the window to each other's soul.
You've been there so long, we've shared so many firsts.
You've seen all my best days and I've seen all your worst.
We've shared tears and tantrums and love and laughter.
Lies and betrayal; fights for and against each other.

We both share the gossip, even when we're not in it.
We argue like enemies but make up in a minute.
We've been distant at times, but always been close.
And we always recoup when you're doing the most.
You've done wrong and so have I.
But that doesn't matter to us.
All that matters is each other.
Through thick and thin.
Through the ups and the downs.
The good, the bad and the ugly;
Until the end of time.

When you've been through it all,
And they're all you can see,
Then, that is when friends become family.

## *Friendship Goals*

I used to want friends to want me.
Now I want friends who want me.
I used to want friends to spend time with me.
Now I want friends who spend time with me.
I used to want friends to like what I like.
Now I want friends who like what I like.
I used to want to be popular.
And now, I'm popular with my friends.

## *Blood is thicker than water*

They say blood is thicker than water.
Then why is it that the blood in some mouths move so loosely?
Why is that a glass of water always seems to be ready when I am thirsty?
If blood is thicker than water, then why is water good for me?
Why does blood get so toxic when it's not supposed to be?

Why is it that the cuts filled with blood cause the most pain?
Why is it that the water clears the wound so we can start once again?
Why is it that when you need the blood the most, it never seems to be there?
But the water flows right out of your tap?

Why does water nourish the blood, even when blood runs like water?
They say blood is thicker than water,
But I remember plenty of times when water was there
And blood wasn't.
So if blood is thicker than water,
I'd rather a thinner consistency.

## *Sisterly love*

I can't help but love you. It runs so deep.

I may love you because of our circumstances

But I love you unconditionally.

You've been a role model in times of uncertainty.

And most times, that's worked out for the best.

Apart from the time you taught me how to smoke

And encouraged me to pop my cherry subconsciously.

Though you probably didn't intend to.

I learnt the best and the worst of my habits directly from you.


You are my second mother. You are my first friend.

You are the best sister I could ever ask for.

You are my pillar of perfection.

You're the only one who truly understands our unique experience and the quirks that make us, "us".


You get the random outbursts in private.

You get the rationale in public.

You get why we don't make a fuss.

You get the constant need for security.

You get all the no nonsense stuff.

You get all the jokes about mothers, fathers and our crazy family.

Our childhood was such a hoot that we'd rather turn a blind eye

Like the night owls trying to make sense of their warped dreams.

Thank you for being there and turning up

Even when you didn't want to.

Thank you for borrowing me the clothes that I stole.

Thank you for lending me the money that I never gave back.

Thank you for finding my marbles when I almost lost them.

Thank you for all that you do.

And if there was ever a choice, I would always choose you.

No doubt.

## *Best Cousins*

Since birth we've grown like two peas in a pod.

Call us forced friends but it works.

What you did, I did. What you had, I wanted.

And we have so much to look back on.

From playing games on the station like Pop Idol and Dance mat.

Playing cricket with the calor gas and making tissue balls to splat.

Eating noodles and frying pancakes

(which I'd save in my night dress)

It was all fun and games

'till we had to clean up the mess.


But we'd beg our parents for sleepovers.

If you didn't ask, then it was me.

Until I had to stay. There was no choice.

No one could look after me.

But you took me in like a friend and treated me like house family.

That's when we dropped the cousin and we became sisters instantly.


12.5% of our DNA is already the same but now it feels like 50.

You are my forgotten twin.

We've evolutionised how we relate.

We used to argue like cat and dog

But now we debate.

We used to lie like a wolf in sheep's clothing

And now we lay our souls bare.

We'd smoke tea, chat shit and sing our hearts out on karaoke.
We're so close I told you the day before I lost my virginity.
Imagine that... You probably don't even remember but that is a fact.

We share secret jokes.
You understand me in ways no one else gets.
You've seen my fears manifest and you've rationalised them all.
You are a role model to me now in so many ways.

With you, I get more than a friend, more than a cousin.
I get an extra sister who I can tell my real secrets to.
I get a frister for life and for that, I thank you.

## *Daddy's Girl*

Anyone can be a father but it takes a special man to be a dad.
I can tell which one you are through the experiences I've had.
You've taken on responsibilities most men would've given away.
When most would've ran, well you chose to stay.

Things were not always pretty and far from perfect.
But deep down in my heart, I know you did your best.
Circumstances slapped you in the face and you stepped right up.
You took it all in your stride, even when things got too much.

Imagine as a man, having to bring up two teenage girls single-handedly.
Homework. Periods. Hormones. Boys. Mischief. And hygiene.
It wasn't easy to say the least but you tackled us like a beast.
Teaching us to question our actions and take responsibility.
You taught us life may not always go our way so resilience is key.

In fact there are so many life skills that you directly taught me.
How to; read, relax, enjoy, love music and be expressive,
Accept people and situations, manage myself, move on and be active,
Be compassionate, be self-reliant, be honest, be logical,
Be responsible, be independent, be realistic, be loyal,
And many more.

I remember, I wanted to be favoured by you so I'd do anything you would want.

But you valued independence of thought so you gave me tough love.

You taught me the value of respect over love and it's safe to say, you did a good job.

You were the first man to model what I should expect

And accept from the opposite sex.

There is a difference.

And for that reason, I am truly blessed

And you made sure that I knew that so I'm thankful for that.

Daddy's little girl always, no matter how big I get.

## *Broken Home*

I was with mum in the week and with dad on the weekends.
So it was boring until Friday when I saw my cousins and friends.
They'd argue when they were together
But get on like a house on fire when they weren't.
She ignored him when they were in the same room
So they were better off separate.

I'd just hang by the window patiently waiting for him to pick me up.
The time dragged like sunken feet
But I refused to let my lids sink like dreams in quick sand.
It was a chance for fun stories, packed with life lessons
And dunking doughnuts dribbled in my hand.
Bike rides. Late nights and mind boggling board games.
Long walks and good conversation.
Visiting family and having sleepovers.
Making songs and dances was our favourite past time.

There wasn't much time for disagreement or misunderstanding,
Like there was in the week.
Because whenever there was a problem,
All I had to do was speak.
I'd get real answers, minus the junk,
Plus a reason for how we got there.
So I could make the sense from nonsense
Whilst I was in his care.

And when it was time to go back to mum's,
Real tears would fill my eyes.
I didn't want to leave my dad all alone,
Plus it's more fun when I was by his side.
'Let it all out,' is what she'd used to say after I came in
And she'd closed the door.
All I wanted was to stay with my daddy.
She never knew what I was crying for.

Sometimes I wonder if it would have been different,
If things were the other way 'round.
With dad in the week and mum on weekends.
Would she have ever let her hair down?

## *Bitter Sweet Mother*

Nobody quite understands me just like how you do.

Because every time I have problem,

You know before I even tell you.

We'll call it a mother's intuition.

But I've never quite figured out whether this is because

I am the thoughts you've instilled.

Or because of our bond since birth.


One things for sure, you gave me a childhood I'll never forget.

I rode the wave in your highs and your lows,

in your elation and your woes

and even in your regrets.

Cheap thrills was your speciality so you drove wildly over the humps.

We'd shout at strangers out of the window.

And sometimes you'd strangle me

or smother a pillow over my face for jokes or just for fun.

And when you were really charged,

you'd blaze music and have late parties of three on a school night.


It seemed like such fun at the time, but somehow,

Now, it just don't seem right.

Now, what words could I use to describe a mother who would do all of this?

Irresponsible. Unsafe. Careless. Reckless. Neglectful.

And maybe, selfish?

But deep down in my heart,

I can now recognise that your intentions were not this.

You were bringing us up the best way you knew how

whilst wrapped up in your reality.

I suppose the knives on the window were to protect us.

And the signs were your freedom of speech.

Those smells must've came from your sense of fear.

And your subconscious just spoke really loudly.

I'm not entirely sure what happened to you

But I know you didn't want it to happen to me.

But I'm still warped from my atypical childhood

So it's hard to know what to believe.

Thoughts created by both my experiences

And my synthetic memory.

I'm ashamed of some of the thoughts that I have,

some I dare not even repeat.

So the things that sound like nonsense,

I have to battle it consciously.

Children are like sponges; they soak it all up

And it seeps out in the most unexpected ways.

Thanks to you, I've learnt logic, rationale, self-care

And that health is real wealth and it definitely pays.

And though you taught me discipline and organisation,

And work must come before play.

You taught me to spend time around people who were light hearted.
And find humour in things that aren't supposed to be funny.
You taught me how to be firm and resilient and also how to live humbly.

Until this very day, you still teach me lessons,
Even though you probably don't mean to.
But I'm still learning how to protect myself
from ending up being just like you.

## *The Matriarch*

The strength of a woman is worth that of a thousand men
And throughout the years you have proved that time and time again.
You've brought forth life 11 times over and we are still counting.
As the seeds you have sown are only just sprouting.

It's taken generations to reach real growth,
Though the lessons were long since planted.
The apple doesn't fall far from the tree,
So my bite is worse than my bark
And it leaves a bittersweet aftertaste.
So only those who can handle the shade will reside under my branches.
And for those who can't handle the heat,
Through the twisting vines of my honesty,
Well, they'll just have to find another tree.

We hibernate in winter, working our flesh to the core,
Just so we can reap the fruits of our labour.
You taught us how to make something out of nothing.
That's why we had inch-high baths.
You taught us how to multiply it until it was enough.
That one dumpling, fed all of us.

You taught us to listen with our eyes and look with our ears.

You taught us loyalty trumps dishonour and bravery trumps fear.

So now, we love one another like we love ourselves

And despite the trauma that we've been through.

Now, we gather at any occasion

And meet up to work things through.

Though you taught us to treat our men like Kings,

You're the true royalty.

You keep the ship afloat.

You lead with your head.

You're top of the hierarchy.

Without you, there'd be nothing.

There'd be no us.

You alone, define matriarchy

## *Grandad: A Man of Distinction*

Grandad: A dad, a granddad, a friend and most importantly
A man of distinction.
Distinct in his style, his strength and his words not to mention.
He commanded attention.
When he walked into a room, you knew he was there.
Known for his cream hat, his suit, his suave debonair.
Tall, brown and handsome, with unusual blue eyes,
and his cheeky little grin; the ladies demise.
Why I'm not surprised.
He was ruthless with his thoughts.
The truth… No Lies.

My Grandad; a man who can.
He would be the first one to say,
"Ole a trade. 'Ave a plan."
His wise words resonate in my soul.
Live in colour, my life goals
"Live for your family, No carry no fren."
Yet granddad had friends, in fact many friends.
In the pub, Domino club;
A man truly known.
With family, with friends but never alone…

"I love you all," is what he used to say.

We knew that he meant it.

He was blunt in every way.

"You cheeky likkle monkey!" he'd cuss when he was vex.

But above all, his family he highly respects.


Grandad; a proud man; he never hesitated to be dedicated

But today his life must be celebrated.

With a 'Wata and Whiskey and 2 cube o' ice.'

C'mon! Family first! No matter the price.

Rest in peace Grandad.

You'll always be remembered in our hearts.

By Nichole Martin and Dionne Walters

## *A Letter to my Future Child*

Though I am keen to meet you,
I'm not ready for you yet.
I'm still preparing things for you,
so your life is as smooth as it gets.
Things have not been easy and this is only the beginning.
Because once I make that decision to create and meet you,
There is no going back again.
Life will throw you with some challenges,
and I want you to be prepared for that.
So many things will test your character,
and so many people will hold you back.
Whilst it is essential we learn from others,
I want you to have strength in your opinion.
Not everyone will hold your best interests at heart,
and I want you to learn to read other people's intentions.
Let your instincts guide you when deciphering
what feels wrong from right.
Don't feel afraid to say 'No,'
even when others try convince you otherwise.
If you want something, go out there and get it
and don't let nobody tell you, you can't.
Make a plan, work hard and stick to it
And surely you'll reach for the stars.
And if you don't, then you must take responsibility
for the cause of your actions.

And when mistakes happen, I hope you find value in the lesson
that you can learn from.
Try new things, see the world and create memories
because in the end, they will always be with you.
Find out what you like and don't like,
so that those decisions can help to guide you.
I'll be there to make sure that you champion
at anything you put your mind to.
And if you fail, you can try and try again,
so you know nothing can ever defeat you.
I may not always be there to hold your hand
but I'll be there to catch you if you fall.
And give you all the cuddles you need
until you're ready to face it all.
But I will not facilitate any neediness
or any irrational fears.
For we must learn to be independent
and not fear what's not really there.
Though my love may seem tough at times,
Please understand I want nothing but the best for you.
But we must all learn from life's lessons.

P.S I will always love you x

# AUTHOR'S NOTES

Thank you for taking the time out to read to the most intimate expression of me. And this collection of poetry is but only the beginning of the journey.
Follow the author and keep up-to-date with the releases of all forth-coming work.

# CONTACT THE AUTHOR

Website: www.djwalterswriter.com
Instagram: djwalterswriter
Twitter: djwalterswriter
Email: djwalterswriter@gmail.com

# ACKNOWLEDGEMENTS

First of all, I would like to thank my mother and father for their ongoing support through my ventures. They have undoubtedly shown patience, loyalty and enthusiasm throughout the entire process and I appreciate them both for all the individual things they have done to allow me to reach this point in my life.

Also, I would like to give thanks to my Sister Shay and my partner Stefan. Behind Those Dark Eyes wouldn't be complete without those two by my side. Both have provided me with the much-needed feedback that has helped to produce the final product of works. They are always offering me the support that I need to progress through my writing journey. Their selflessness is incomparable and I will be forever grateful for the input I have received from them. And also my cousins, Tanya, Ricky, Chanelle and Nichole who have given me advice along the way. My family are truly my backbone and I appreciate them all.

Additionally, I would like to thank my friends Laila, Krystal and Pinar who've listened and read parts of this novel and given me constructive feedback. Your opinions have helped to shape poems in ways words can't describe.

Furthermore, I would like to thank all those who have supported my journey and shown an ongoing interest in my new ventures. I truly appreciate each and every review that I have received and the ongoing love that has been spread through social media. Since publishing, I have been able to network with a variety of people from all walks of life and this has been mainly through the use of the internet. I appreciate the support of every single one of you and I pray that the word continues to spread even further.

And last but not least, I would like to thank the country lockdown for giving me the brain space to produce these musings of work. If it wasn't for this extra time, I wouldn't have been able to produce these pieces with such thought behind them. For that, I am truly grateful.

# ABOUT THE AUTHOR

Dionne Jennene Walters, the author of The Vacation Lodge series, is a captivating erotic novelist who was born and raised in South London, England. Studying at both City University and Goldsmiths University, she has achieved qualifications in Sociology, Criminology and Education. Her studies have helped her develop an intricate understanding of people, behaviour, motives and the way that we learn. As a young child, Walters always showed a strong interest in the performing arts and poetry. And her work as a teacher re-ignited her passion for performances and creative writing that had the ability to capture the audience's attention. Walters holds a strong belief in the power behind words. When they are used wisely, she believes words can excite, inspire and enable anyone to get whatever they desire in life.

www.ingramcontent.com/pod-product-compliance
Lightning Source LLC
Chambersburg PA
CBHW030522080526
44586CB00011B/294